Great
Australian
Catholics

EDMUND
CAMPION

Aurora Books
David Lovell Publishing

First published in 1997 by
Aurora Books
300 Victoria Street
Richmond Victoria 3121

in association with
David Lovell Publishing
PO Box 822
Ringwood Victoria 3134

Cover photograph by Brian Millgate
Editorial & design by David Lovell
Print production by Sylvana Scannapiego
Typeset in 10.5/13 Century Old Style
Printed in Australia

National Library of Australia
Cataloguing-in-Publication data:

Campion, Edmund.
  Great Australian Catholics
  Includes index.
  ISBN 1 86355 057 7.

  1. Catholic Church - Australia - History. 2. Catholics -
  Australia - Biography. 3. Catholics - Australia - History.
  I. Title
282.092294

Acknowledgements: The material in this book first appeared as
articles in *Messenger* and *Madonna* magazines and appears here
courtesy of the publisher of those magazines.

Contents

Introduction

WHEN I GO TO MASS in the Sydney cathedral, I like to sit where the 19th century building joins the 20th century addition. It appears to be a seamless join, although if you know where to stand, your foot can feel the millimetre or two rise in the floor which betrays the joining of the seams.

That is a good place for a historian to sit, where you can feel the continuity and the change between one century and the next. From there, too, you can see the bank of windows which tell the early history of the people who worship in this place. Here is the first official Mass, in 1803, celebrated by a convict priest. The next window shows Catholic laity praying before the Blessed Sacrament left in their care by a priest expelled in 1818. Then there is the laying of the cathedral's foundation stone in 1821 by Governor Lachlan Macquarie, who gave St Mary's its name. A fourth window shows the arrival of the first bishop, John Bede Polding, in 1835.

There's a pleasing mix-up in some of these windows. One of the inscriptions has to be read back to front; and on the other side of the cathedral aisle a papal guard and two monsignori have swapped places with a group of the Sydney laity, who look out of place and, to my eyes, somewhat confused at the Pope's court in Rome, while the Roman *apparatchiks*, whose places they have taken, look decidedly uncomfortable in 19th century Sydney. The mix-up in the windows is a reminder that even cathedral authorities can make mistakes.

As I sit waiting for Mass, my eye travels up the sandstone

columns and walls to the bases of the arches along the aisles and around the windows. There are people's heads carved there, 150 in all. Some of them are so striking that you are sure the stonecarvers had individual models in mind; many, on the other hand, are types: a monk, a nun, a workman, a housewife. Well, if they were once identifiable, their names are now lost to us, so that they represent to my imagination the anonymous makers of the Catholic story in Australia.

Modern historians, such as Portia Robinson, are evaporating some of that anonymity and giving us a surer picture of our forefathers and foremothers. They show, for instance, that the society of a second chance which began here two centuries ago was founded on stable relationships that in reality, if not on paper, must be called successful families.

For too long historians have followed the infamous lead given by the Reverend Samuel Marsden, who drew up a list of colonial women in 1804, putting more than 1000 of them under the heading 'concubines', alongside fewer than 400 'wives'. Reality seems different from this moralistic view. It suggests a happier outline of our story: crime in the past ... paid for ... then a new beginning ... with a stable line of work, blossoming into a true and real family which endured and gave a permanent foundation to the society of the future which became Australia.

Many of these foundational families were Catholic—a reminder that the first Australian Catholics were lay people. They brought their religion with them, kept it alive somehow, passed it on to their children and nurtured it. No one claims hothouse levels of piety among those first Catholics. That would be bad history; but to ignore them is bad history, too.

In cultural characteristics this religion may have been closer to Italian Catholicism than to the legalistic, clericalist Irish-Australian Catholicism many of us once knew well. The Catholic faith in early Australia was a poem that gave life meaning or respite. It was a vision that ennobled the future and gave

2

one the spiritual means to sustain the present. It was also a folk culture shared with others, a bond of loyalty. And it was *there*.

Surgeon Peter Cunningham, who travelled out on five voyages with convict ships, wrote that the only signs of religion he had ever seen on the ships were among Catholics, whom he observed unostentatiously 'counting their beads and crossing themselves and repeating their prayers from the book'.

Among those who write about colonial religion there is a tension between a kind of subfusc Lutheranism, which sees faith as the decisive element, and a sort of secularised Calvinism, for which salvation is somehow evidenced by respectability and proper table manners. I incline to the Lutheran view. There is certainly enough evidence to suggest that faith, unsupported by much ecclesiastical apparatus, struck roots here and, at the very least, stayed alive.

Thus in 1819, one year before the arrival of the official priests Conolly and Therry, a French scientific corvette, *L'Uranie*, put into Sydney Harbour for rest and recreation. Its chaplain, the Abbé de Quelen, was run off his feet by importunate colonial Catholics who sought the sacraments, spiritual counsel and direction from him. Another piece of evidence comes from the first official census, in 1828. The census found that 20 per cent of adults born here claimed the name Catholic. This is a precious statistic because it offers us a window on to a lost world when the Catholic Church in Australia consisted solely of lay people. Each one of that 20 per cent was born here, nurtured here, brought up here and given a religious identity here *before* the coming of the priests in 1820.

Even the youngest of these adults would have been twelve or thirteen before the priests came; yet they claimed the Catholic name. How had this happened? The answer must lie in those Catholic households, where, whatever Samuel Marsden might say, stable family relationships were established, family traditions and stories were passed on and family religious cultures were nourished.

The coming of the priests brought change. In the 19th century the domestic history of Catholicism in Australia followed the domestic history of Catholicism in Ireland. There, as here, the century opened with a loose, ramshackle, bits-and-pieces, unclerical people's religion which was warmly hospitable to the marvellous, the mysterious and at times the superstitious.

Throughout the 19th century this rich, living popular religion was transformed by the priests; so that it became the Catholicism most of us knew until just the other day: parochial, disciplined, observant, dutiful, obedient, fearful, guilty and sin-obsessed; and also celebratory, colourful, comforting, heart-stirring, intelligent, pastoral and, in the best sense, sacramental—for it saw the impress of the divine underneath and behind the whole created world. It too was a poem. The locale of the old Catholicism had been the people's homes; that of this new Catholicism was the parish church, where the priest was. If the first period can be called frontier or colonial Catholicism, the name of the second is parish Catholicism.

Father John Joseph Therry, the undisciplined but deeply loved pioneer, links the two periods. In 1820 he came to a frontier church. When he died, in the Balmain parish presbytery in 1864, there was a cathedral in Sydney, dioceses and parishes across the continent and a Catholic directory advertising regular hours for Mass, devotions and confessions. Frontier Catholicism was long past; this was now a parochial religion.

Most of the people in this book lived in this middle period. The silence or paucity of the historical record defeats attempts to put many names or faces to the story of the first Catholics. Those who lived between them and the Vatican II generation who will read this book are easier to track, even if their tracks lead to places unfamiliar to ecclesiastical historians. They deserve to be remembered.

Seen from this distance, their outstanding religious characteristic was devotion, especially devotion to the Blessed Sacrament. At its peak this saw someone like the Scripture

professor at Manly, William Leonard, who I think was a genuine mystic. Immobile and speechless on Fridays, he seemed to share physically the sufferings of Christ in the Passion.

Lower levels of the seven storied mountain were more heavily populated. So, for example, priests who were at the Sydney cathedral during World War II spoke for the rest of their lives about the intensity, the *presence* of film cameraman Damien Parer before the altar. One gets insights into a lay man's religious life from the prisoner of war diaries of Stan Arneil. His diaries show the matter of fact, everyday reality of the religion of an ordinary young parishioner swept up in the fall of Singapore. Testimony to the everydayness of laymen's religion comes from another Burma Railway POW diarist, Jim Lynch, who several times records his Sunday activities with two words: 'Communion … poker'.

The best place to explore this lay Catholic religious life is in the writings of 'Miriam Agatha'. She was a Queensland schoolteacher, her real name Agatha Le Breton, who wrote the children's pages of the *Messenger* and *Annals* for 60 years before Vatican II. There is an entry on her in the *Oxford Companion to Australian Children's Literature* but it doesn't tell you much. I wrote about her in *Australian Catholics* and there is a profile of her in this book; I wish we knew more. The generations of children who read her monthly stories and columns were led gently into the culture of Catholic practice. This skilled writer, better than any other, impressed on youthful imaginations the attractions of parish Catholicism. From 'Miriam Agatha' they learned about praying in November for the Holy Souls in Purgatory, honouring Mary in May and the Sacred Heart in June, visiting the Blessed Sacrament, making the Stations of the Cross, keeping the nine First Fridays, patron saints, guardian angels, rosary beads, medals, statues and crucifixes. Her writings are a rich archive, largely unexplored, of the mentality and imaginative world of the church of her time.

If you look for the seed beds of the tenacious devotional

strain of parish Catholicism, you will swiftly arrive at the parish school. Staffed from the local convent, the parish school is the central institution of this story. Through their schools, nuns became the single most creative force in Catholic history. By 1910 there were more than 5000 teaching sisters in Australia, a formidable force outnumbering the priests. Before state aid, much of parish life revolved round the school. It had to be built and paid for, staffed, repaired and supported. Doing all this gave a parish its social life, for it meant raffles, bazaars, balls, dances, house parties, chocolate wheels, bingo games, tennis competitions and anything else you could think of that might raise money for the school.

As well as the parish school, religious offered secondary education, often in boarding schools in the country. Boarding schools were a significant element in Catholic culture, linking important networks of past pupils. As their histories get written, we are being offered a view from the desks of previously self-effacing creators of a sub-culture. It is fortunate too that reticence about self, a product of the modesty officially enjoined on the good nun or brother, is now giving way to a healthy frankness which must delight historians. Just in time, their stories are being told by themselves, in books like Anne Henderson's *Mary MacKillop's Sisters* and Naomi Turner's *Which Seeds Shall Grow?* The high human cost of this enterprise needs to be remembered, which is why I have written here about Sister Dolores White OP, who died in a psychiatric hospital, aged 37.

Another mark of parish Catholicism was the proliferation of parish organisations, from sodalities and confraternities to sporting bodies, dramatic societies, debating unions and social clubs. They seemed to cover every activity. Most of them were inward looking, meeting the needs of parishioners and, perhaps as an intended consequence, isolating them from the wider civil community. So one sometimes comes across the phrase 'ghetto Catholicism' to describe this period. This may not be entirely fair. After all, the Society of St Vincent de Paul is a

mainstream organisation of this era; and, as the profile of its
Australian founder, Charles Gordon O'Neill, makes plain, it
served the whole community, not just Catholics.

Again, many members of parish organisations used them
as stepping stones to activity in the wider community. Reading
lives of Catholic politicians, one is struck by the number of them
who learned public speaking in parish debating unions.
Similarly, you find many Catholic office-holders in community
bodies who learned their organisational skills in the parish. For
that matter, not every Catholic body was parish based. The
Catholic Women's Social Guild and St Joan's Alliance, two feminist groups which turn up in several profiles, had lives outside
parish boundaries.

Mention of them alerts one to another characteristic of this
era, its strong interest in social justice. Social justice is a hazy
term; it stands here for a perception of wrongs in society and a
willingness to be active in righting those wrongs, whether the
focus be Aborigines or women or workers. An interest in social
justice may have sprung from a feeling that you yourself were
getting the rough end of the pineapple. Plenty of Catholics felt
like that—it had something to do with the denial of state aid
and those advertisements which said, 'Catholics need not
apply'.

The advertisements, of course, had much to do with how
you lined up on the British Empire: RCs were thought to be
'disloyal'. This is the reason why their heroes were men like
Daniel Mannix and Maurice O'Reilly, who spoke up for them in
public, or sporting stars like Les Darcy, Stan McCabe and Bill
O'Reilly, who took a few knocks because they were 'different'.
The great question of Australian identity was being fought out
in Reformation terms and the Reformation divide ran deep
through all Australian society. The world of ecumenism lay
somewhere in the future.

That future, however, was on the way. To anyone who could
read the signals, lay apostolate movements pointed the way for-

ward. Catholicism was coming out of the ghetto. Fifty years ago movements like the Young Christian Workers and the university Newman Societies tried to form a new-style Catholic laity. The apostolate put the Bible into the laity's hands, especially the New Testament, encouraging a biblical mentality. It brought them closer to the Mass and made the liturgy the wellspring of people's spirituality. It developed their social conscience through reading and discussion of topical writers and papal encyclicals. It made them self-reliant as Catholics and loosened clerical controls. It opened their minds to new ideas, not all of them with a church provenance.

The universities were test beds of the lay apostolate. From 1950, commonwealth scholarships had opened universities to more young Catholics. Those scholarships were a key element in the Australian Catholic story, for they enabled great numbers of Catholics to move into the professions, thus changing the demographics (and in time the politics) of Australian Catholicism. University experience introduced Catholics to unfamiliar ideas and principles, such as the liberal principle of free speech. As well, the Catholic culture experienced at university was somewhat different from the culture of the parishes. Clergy and laity were closer together, so that there was a ready acceptance of lay leadership. Ecumenism, congregational liturgy, openness to Australian culture, biblical spirituality—such were the waves of the future already being experienced in lay apostolate groups at the universities.

Another major cultural shift came with the massive intakes of migrants after World War II. In Australian historiography Catholic too often means Irish; yet there was never a time when Catholics of non-English-speaking backgrounds were not in the picture. The tens of thousands who came here after World War II significantly changed that picture. They claimed the Catholic name yet refused to identify as Irish Australians. To those brought up to equate Catholic and Irish—who thought the Irish way was the only authentic way to be a Catholic—this was an

affront; and tensions were inevitable.

It was a hard lesson but the newcomers taught old Irish Australians that there were many different ways of being Catholic, all authentic. Thus they taught us pluralism and created a multicultural Catholic community, mirroring what was happening in the wider community. Slowly a realisation was dawning that there was a distinction between religion and religious culture. This realisation was crucial because it prepared us to take on board the huge cultural transformations which historians have code-named 'Vatican II'. For Vatican II was much more than a meeting of bishops who issued various documents on church affairs. Rather, it was a profound transformation of mentality and culture over several decades which saw the displacement of much of the religious culture that had been carried over from the Middle Ages.

It is still too early to say much about this third period in Australian Catholic history, the Vatican II era. Several features, however, are already apparent, and they can be seen in some of the profiles in this book. Catechists who teach religion in government schools have opened up a new chapter in our story. Numbered in thousands, they have taken responsibility for one of the central ministries in the church, handing on the faith. Alongside them stand the lay men and women who now staff Catholic schools, formerly the province of nuns and brothers.

Their teaching has strengthened and deepened their own appreciation of the faith; and their demands for intellectual nourishment have produced the current boom in adult education and a regrowth of Catholic publishing. This development of new ministries is matched by ministerial experimentation by members of religious orders. Once, religious life was structured round one or two occupations; now, it is a launch into radical freedoms.

One of the most surprising novelties of the Vatican II era has been a change in styles of leadership. What is noticeable about the new leaders is that they are encouragers—that, more

than anything else, is what makes them different from the leaders of the past. Ann Clark, who died as this book was being prepared for press and who occupies its final pages, was an outstanding example of the new leadership emerging in Australian Catholicism. Above all, she was a great encourager.

I began this introduction sitting in the cathedral, waiting for Sunday Mass to begin. One of the first things I do is to see what hymns will be sung. Like everyone else, I have my likes and dislikes. It is a good day when I see from the bulletin that we will be singing Walter Chalmers Smith's old hymn *Immortal, invisible*, for it has two lines that resonate throughout the day:

> And so let Thy glory, Almighty, impart
> Through Christ in the story, Thy Christ to the heart.

This collection of profiles tries to delineate Christ in the Australian Catholic story. I thank the successive editors of the *Messenger* and *Madonna* magazines who have given house room to these writings over the years. I thank too those readers who have encouraged me to continue in this line of country and who urged me to make this collection. In a special way it is their book, which I now offer back to them.

In particular, I dedicate this book of 'Christ in the story' to my dear sister (Doreen) Mary Campion OP. Her faithful life as a Dominican sister has shown countless thousands, more winningly than any writing of mine can do, the eternal attractiveness of the Christ in her heart.

Edmund Campion
Catholic Institute of Sydney
Easter 1997

Madame Virtue and the Abbé

ROSE DE FREYCINET

SHE WAS PRETTY, YOUNG and very much in love with her husband. So when the Navy ordered her husband away on a long scientific voyage, Rose de Freycinet made up her mind to go with him. She had her hair cut, got dressed as a sailor and was smuggled aboard ship the night before sailing. It was against Navy regulations but Louis de Freycinet was the captain, so he thought he might chance it. Their ship, *L'Uranie*, would be away from France for more than three years.

On their long circumnavigation of the globe Rose was often bored. She kept to their cabin most of the time, practising the guitar, writing up her journal and learning English. At sea, she longed to pick flowers and she dreamed of farmyard chickens, milk and eggs. Headaches plagued her. Whenever she went on deck the crew dropped their voices respectfully but soon their oaths and off-colour songs got louder and drove her back to the cabin. She was a modest woman. At a ball in Mauritius her refusal to follow extreme fashions in dress

earned her the nickname Madame Virtue.

Her only friend was the chaplain, Abbé de Quelen, 'a respectable ecclesiastic' as she told her mother. In his mid-fifties, he had survived the Revolution by taking the oath of conformity, although forced to appear once before a revolutionary tribunal. On the restoration of Bourbon power he kept his post as chaplain to a female prison and mental asylum. Then his uncle, the Archbishop of Paris, managed his appointment as a canon of the royal Abbey of St Denis and so he came to be on board *L'Uranie*.

Despite the years of irreligion during the Revolution, Rose noticed that the sailors were devout in their attendance at Mass. Her letters home carried descriptions of Holy Week ceremonies in Spanish territories and the baptism of a leading official in the Sandwich Islands attended by the pagan King, the royal wives and his court.

The chaplain suffered from scurvy, which restricted his pastoral work. When the ship sprung a leak, however, he took his turn at the pumps and helped keep the men jolly. He also found time to pray with Rose, who was terrified. Ten hours later, when they had survived this shipwreck, he set up a Marian altar on shore and all sang a *Te Deum*. In their extreme destitution his hair powder came in handy, for they made 'bread' from it, which Rose said was edible if eaten while hot.

The shipwreck occurred on their way home from Australia. After exploring Western Australia—where Rose may have been the first white woman to land—they arrived in Sydney Harbour in November 1819. Captain de Freycinet had been there 17 years earlier and he surprised his wife by anchoring at night. At dawn, when she awoke, Sydney spread itself before her delighted eyes.

The people of Sydney welcomed their French visitors with luncheons, balls and dinners—although on their first night

ashore the de Freycinets lost their table linen and silver to a burglar. Governor Lachlan Macquarie tried to reimburse them but the Captain said no, it was their own fault.

Abbé de Quelen found unexpected work in Sydney. The Catholics there, who numbered about one-third of the 11,000 inhabitants, had been without a priest since the deportation of the unstable and unofficial Father Jeremiah O'Flynn in May 1818.

Officially these priestless Catholics came under the oversight of the Reverend Samuel Marsden, government chaplain. But many of them refused to acknowledge his spiritual authority. They did not want his baptisms, nor his marriages, nor would they send their children to his schools, which they saw as engines of proselytism.

Whatever their crimes in the past, these colonial Catholics entered into stable, lasting relationships and founded permanent families. Now that they had a priest among them again, if only for five weeks, they were anxious to seek him out. Writing to her mother, Rose said the Abbé was in demand for baptisms and marriages. Also, she wrote, he gave them instruction and spiritual direction and many came on board for Sunday Mass.

The names of these lay people have been lost, probably in the shipwreck. Although nameless, they remain a precious element in the Australian Catholic story because they were the true foundations on whom later generations would build.

A tradition
in voice

CATHERINE FITZPATRICK

THE CHOIR OF ST MARY'S CATHEDRAL, Sydney, is a link with the earliest days of Catholicism in this country. It goes back to the time when there were no priests in Australia and the faith was nurtured and passed on by mothers and fathers in their families. The first Australian Catholics were lay people without priests.

Such was Catherine Fitzpatrick, wife of a convict who later became chief bailiff of the Supreme Court. The Fitzpatricks came to Sydney in 1811 and by the end of the decade Mrs Fitzpatrick was running a Catholic school. Her own sons were among the pupils, to whom she taught the catechism and how to serve Mass.

Suddenly, in 1818, without warning, a priest arrived. This was Father Jeremiah O'Flynn, a former missionary who had credentials from Rome but no permission from the British government. He claimed that his government papers were coming on a later ship and in the meantime he

promised Governor Lachlan Macquarie not to officiate as a priest.

It is now clear that Father O'Flynn broke his promise and conducted a clandestine ministry. He was a fluent Gaelic speaker, which was balm to the many convicts whose first language was Gaelic, not English. He also began to make converts among the soldiers. Macquarie became incensed at the priest's insubordination and after a few months had him arrested and deported. O'Flynn took the story of the priestless colony back to Ireland, inspiring others to follow his lead.

During his months in Sydney the Catholics had rallied round him. It seems that Catherine Fitzpatrick gathered together a choir to sing at the priest's Masses. When he was deported he left behind the Blessed Sacrament at a Catholic home in Kent Street and this became a continuing centre of Catholic devotion. Here a men's sodality kept watch before the Blessed Sacrament. On Sundays Catholics came there for prayers and readings from the Mass. Mrs Fitzpatrick's choir sang Vespers and other liturgical music there.

So when the first official priests, Fathers Philip Conolly and John Joseph Therry, arrived in 1820, they found a choral tradition already established among Australian Catholics. Therry was a music-lover who did not like celebrating Mass without music. The choir sang at his Masses in the local courthouse, at times augmented by members of regimental bands stationed in Sydney. When disputes split the Catholic community, Mrs Fitzpatrick's choir stuck with Father Therry and followed him to the chapel he then built.

They had sung at the laying of the foundation stone of St Mary's Cathedral by Governor Macquarie in 1821 and became the cathedral choir when that building came into regular use in 1833. So they were ready for the arrival of the first bishop, John Bede Polding osb, in 1835. The bishop was astonished

by the quality of their singing, saying that he had not expected to hear a Mozart Mass in Botany Bay.

With the coming of the Benedictines the choir extended its range. It gave the first choral concert in the colony, featuring movements from Handel's *Messiah* and Haydn's *The Creation*. Later 'firsts' would include Beethoven's *Mass in C*, Rossini's *Stabat Mater* and Edward Elgar's *Dream of Gerontius*. Bishop Polding wrote to a friend in 1838, 'we have Mozart's or Haydn's music every Sunday'.

The Benedictines insisted that theirs should be a liturgical choir, so women were dismissed. Thus the founder, Mrs Fitzpatrick, faded from the scene as clerics took control of music at the cathedral. In time, however, laymen once more became directors of the choir and women, often professional artists, began to sing with the choir again.

The greatest of the 19th century musical directors seems to have been John Albert Delany. When he died in 1907 his tombstone carried the opening bars of one of his Masses and the accolade, 'Australia's most gifted Harmonist and Composer'. Elgar thought him so famous that he sent a cable addressed simply 'Delany—Sydney'. Delany's music is still occasionally sung but the taste for showy operatic Masses has passed.

A modern worshipper at St Mary's Cathedral will hear religious music, not as a concert piece, but as part of a living liturgy. In praying with the cathedral choir, the worshipper makes contact with a choral tradition now more than 175 years old, linking today's Catholic to the priestless days of Mrs Catherine Fitzpatrick.

Pennies from heaven

JOHN SULLIVAN

BEHIND EVERY PARISH PRIEST sits a banker. Well, you cannot run the church on Hail Marys alone, as St Paul knew. The parish priest is responsible for the parish plant. If he is to maintain, build, repair and extend the parish buildings, he needs money. Hence, the banker.

Australia's first official priest, Father John Joseph Therry, found this out the hard way. When he arrived in 1820 with his companion and superior, Father Philip Conolly, there were six or seven thousand Catholics in the colony. One of their first needs, the priests decided, was a church; so they set about raising money. In October 1821 Governor Lachlan Macquarie laid the foundation stone of what was to become St Mary's Cathedral in Sydney, the mother church of Australian Catholics.

By then, however, Father Conolly had made his way to Van Diemen's Land, where he would live out his remaining 15 years. Alone on the mainland, Father Therry represented for

many people the Catholic Church. In their generosity they gave him money, making no distinctions whether they were making donations to Father Therry or to the church. To tell the truth, Father Therry himself didn't seem clear on the matter. He had had a sketchy theological education and he carried in his mind no sharp distinction (such as a canon lawyer might expect) between what belonged to him and what belonged to the church.

Confusion was confounded by jumbled book-keeping. His accounts and financial jottings on stray pieces of paper are a spider's web of money coming in, going out, being cross-lent, cross-borrowed, promised, guaranteed, added up, subtracted, minuted and forgotten. It was a banker's nightmare.

The man who had to make sense of that nightmare was John O'Sullivan. Arriving in Sydney in 1828, the 26-year-old Cork man lodged with Father Therry. The housekeeper was Mrs Dwyer, widow of Irish patriot Michael Dwyer. Also there was her daughter Bridget, whom O'Sullivan would marry in 1839. As a child, Bridget had been taken to pray at the cottage where the itinerant Father O'Flynn had left the Blessed Sacrament in 1818 before being deported. She gave her husband a sense of early Australian Catholic history, when the faith had been kept alive by Catholic families before there were any priests.

In Sydney, O'Sullivan became a bank clerk. Moving to Goulburn, he became manager of the local branch of the Commercial Banking Company. Archivist C. J. Duffy has called him Australia's pioneer Catholic bank manager. If that is so, he was the first of a long line of bankers who have helped parish priests through their money difficulties. For O'Sullivan became Father Therry's banker and financial agent.

By now, Father Therry was in Van Diemen's Land, sent there by Bishop Polding to try to soften Father Conolly's

anger against church authority. In his absence from Sydney, which was to be longer than he expected, Father Therry put John O'Sullivan in charge of his affairs. It was a fidgeting responsibility because the priest made sudden calls for money, loans and urgent bail-outs. Back and forward went the letters: What had happened to Father Therry's cattle? Had they strayed? Been taken to market? But where was the money? 'Do not forget to help the poor widow O'Brien of Campbelltown', ran one of his notes. Through it all, the banker kept a calm affection for his ageing friend.

John O'Sullivan got on well with the clergy, without being subservient. Polding and his vicar-general would stay with him on pastoral visits, as did the great archdeacon John McEncroe. He was a generous contributor to their building funds, especially the cathedral. When the Mercy Sisters came to Goulburn, he gave 400 guineas for their fares and took them into his own home until the convent was ready.

Father Therry always remained first in John O'Sullivan's estimation. On the archpriest's death, it fell to his banker to sort out the muddle of his last will and testament. Most of his money he left to bring Irish Jesuits to Australia—the Archbishop couldn't believe it. 'He must have been mad', he expostulated. Nevertheless, the banker steered the will to its destined port; and so the Irish Jesuits came to Melbourne in 1865. It was a final act in a lifetime of caring for Father Therry's interests.

Open
to all

JOHN HUBERT PLUNKETT

WHEN THE AUSTRALIAN CATHOLIC UNIVERSITY set up the John Plunkett Centre for Ethics, people were puzzled by the choice of name. Who was Plunkett? What was his connection with ethics? Why name a research centre after him?

John Hubert Plunkett was an Irishman who came to Sydney in 1832, at the age of thirty. In 1829 Catholic Emancipation had enabled men like Plunkett to aspire to higher positions in the civil service of the British Empire and he became the first law officer of New South Wales. He was right hand man to the liberal Anglican Governor, Sir Richard Bourke.

Plunkett drafted Bourke's historic Church Act of 1836, by which Anglican hegemony was displaced. Previously, the Anglican Church had rights to one-seventh of all land in the colony to fund its churches and schools. Bourke thought that, given the religious mix in Australia, this would surely lead to dissension. Plunkett's Act gave rough-and-ready equality to

the major denominations, granting them government funding according to the numbers of their adherents. Thus the churches, as major communal institutions in a new society, were able to establish themselves and grow towards the future. By the end of his life, however, Plunkett had come to think that the time for such state aid was over.

The spectre of convictism still hung over this new society. Plunkett championed the rights of convicts against arbitrary punishment by their masters. He limited the extent of flogging and the administration of justice in private houses. Local magistrates were essential to the justice system but they were too often amenable to local pressure and inconsistent in their judgments. Plunkett raised their standards, made them accountable and effected greater uniformity in their courts. He thus made equality before the law a possibility.

As liberals, he and Governor Bourke were determined that once a convict had served his time or been freed, he should be able to rejoin society. Nevertheless, belief in 'the convict stain' was widespread. Leaders of society held that an ex-convict was a second class person, forever tainted. This was a form of secularised Calvinism, dividing the world into the socially damned and the saved. The test was jury service. Could ex-convicts serve on a jury? Against opposition Plunkett established the right of ex-convict citizens to become jurors. It was another step towards a just and equal society.

Plunkett's passion for justice is seen at its best in the Myall Creek massacre, when eleven whites seized more than two dozen Aborigines, tied them together with greenhide rope and shot, knifed or hacked them to death. The evidence of murder seemed obvious; yet, on the difficulty of identifying such dismembered corpses, a jury rapidly returned a verdict of Not Guilty.

Plunkett was appalled. Beneath the legal technicalities he

knew there lay the poisonous philosophy that Aborigines were not truly human. They could not as yet give evidence in court—he would try to rectify that, to no avail—and many whites thought of them as pests which should be exterminated. By contrast, Plunkett thought of them as fellow human beings, with the common rights of every human being. As Attorney General, therefore, he moved for a second trial, at which seven white men were found guilty and sentenced to hang. His courage drew on him the hatred of white racists, who demanded his dismissal and made him the scapegoat of their guilty consciences. On the other hand, those who believed in the sacredness of human life and the equality of all before the law saluted him as a hero.

These are some of the reasons for naming an ethics research centre after him. There is another reason. The Plunkett Centre is located at St Vincent's Hospital, Sydney, the first hospital of the Sisters of Charity in Australia. When they arrived in Sydney in 1838, Plunkett met the pioneer sisters on the wharf. Their friend for life, he became treasurer of the hospital building fund and a trustee of the hospital. What appealed to him about St Vincent's Hospital was that it was open to all, with no religious tests before admission.

In time the Sisters of Charity would clash with diocesan authorities over this policy. Plunkett stood by the sisters. He was a good Catholic but no lickspittle of the clergy. Naming a centre for ethics after him today is a worthy honour for this great Australian Catholic.

A patient pioneer

Mother URSULA FRAYNE

Ursula Frayne is one of the best-known religious sisters in Australian history. Founder of the famous school in Nicholson Street, Fitzroy, in Melbourne, her name justly appears in histories of education and in collections of prominent Australian women. But her early years were a rigorous preparation for this fame.

She came to Australia in 1846, as mother superior of the first Sisters of Mercy community in Perth. Arriving in January after 114 days at sea, the seven Irishwomen were struck by the heat. During the day they stayed indoors, venturing out in the evenings to visit the sick and instruct adults. Even so, they could not wear their normal attire.

There were snakes to frighten them, cramped accommodation and monotonous food. Within six months one of them would die. They all missed home and watched, month by month, for mail ships that never seemed to come. Still, they

were young—all except one were under 30—and buoyed up by missionary zeal.

Their youth was one of Mother Frayne's problems. Far from the mother house in Dublin, she had to form and lead her sisters in the religious life. Priests were scarce, so retreats and days of recollection were conducted from books. The young superior sorely missed someone with whom to discuss her tasks.

The eldest of the sisters gave her particular trouble. She was a recent entrant into the convent who, it seems clear, would have benefited from a more settled and regular formation at home. Instead, travel and the demands of the mission took their tolls on her spiritual life. She felt she was not appreciated or trusted to do things her way. She sulked and asked to be sent home. In time she got over it, ending her days 30 years later still as a Mercy Sister, and still in Perth. But it was a cross Ursula Frayne and the pioneers could have done without.

Then there were problems connected with their apostolate. When recruiting them in Ireland, Bishop Brady had told them there were thousands of children in Western Australia waiting to be taught. But when they opened a school only six children turned up, and after a year there were still only 75. Where were the thousands? asked Ursula Frayne. Loftily the bishop replied, 'Out of the stones Almighty God could raise up children to Abraham'.

Attempts to attract fee-paying pupils, who could subsidise the teaching of the poor, were not a great success. Strapped for cash, the sisters spent every spare moment making articles for bazaars and raffles. They were never far from financial danger—although not as bad as the diocese itself, which ran up such huge debts that Bishop Brady was replaced by orders from Rome.

The bishop was Ursula Frayne's greatest trial. A lonely man who lived in a little cubby in the church belfry, open to all weather, he was at first charming to the sisters. He would spend six hours a day chatting at the convent and accepting meals. But Perth lacked sufficient Catholics to warrant a bishop, even one who lived in a belfry. As his financial worries worsened, Bishop Brady worked off his frustrations on the Sisters of Mercy.

When Mother Frayne asked him to spend less time at the convent so that they could get on with their work, he flew into a rage. His innate bossiness now came to the fore, as he interfered in the day-to-day running of the convent. Written permission was required from him for the slightest changes. He inspected all bills and receipts.

If a sister failed to ask his blessing whenever she saw him, he considered her lacking in respect. Asking permission to leave the recreation room while he was there was a mark of contempt. Any infringement (as he saw it) of his wishes was called insubordination. One of the sisters wrote glumly home to Ireland, 'God is our only protection in Australia'.

Bishop Brady's replacement, Bishop Jose Serra, a Spanish Benedictine, proved to be in the same mould. He ordered them to remove from the school any books that were not to his taste. Every movement between their two convents required his permission. He exacted minute obedience under threats of canon law penalties.

Ursula Frayne left for Melbourne in 1857. Her eleven years in the west had been a testing novitiate for the great mother superior.

A struggle for justice

J. K. HEYDON

JOHN BEDE POLDING IS A REVERED FIGURE among Australian Catholics. The bicentenary of his birth on 18 November 1794 was an occasion for remembering the saintly qualities of Australia's first Catholic bishop. As novice master at Downside Abbey in England he had pictured to his novices the possibilities of the Australian mission. They could be, he said, like Benedictine monks of the Dark Ages, travelling vast distances by horse or by foot with a Mass kit on their backs and so they would bring Christ to a new continent.

Sure enough, when he came to Australia as a 40-year-old bishop in 1835, this is what he loved to do. He would leave Sydney and paperwork behind to strike out on long missionary safaris, rounding up stray Catholics as he went.

In and around Sydney Polding's favourite work was with the convicts. The government agreed that their first week in Sydney could be spent at the cathedral. There Polding and his priests catechised them, heard their confessions and gathered

them round the altar. Through this unique apostolate thousands came to Christ. For decades afterwards many of them called their sons Bede to show their gratitude for his pastoral care.

But a great, even saintly, priest does not always make a good bishop. Polding's episcopal strategy depended on getting enough English monks to make it a success, and this was never likely. As well, most of the Catholics in Australia were Irish; they liked the Irish secular priests who came out to serve them. To them, the archbishop's Benedictines-first policy seemed unjust. Non-Benedictine religious orders who came to Sydney had a hard time and did not stay.

It was not only Irish Catholics who thought the Benedictine policy unjust. An example was Jabez King Heydon, who had emigrated from England as a young man with his wife and family. Heydon, a Methodist, read Newman and discussed religion with the pioneer Catholic journalist, W. A. Duncan, a Scottish convert. Under these influences he became a Catholic (his wife followed him 21 years later). In 1857, Heydon took over the *Freeman's Journal* and persuaded Duncan to write for him.

The *Freeman* gave dissatisfied Catholics a forum for airing their disapproval of diocesan policy. Half the Catholics could not read or write, as the 1856 census showed. No wonder, said the critics, when there were not enough schools. Polding hit back by getting the other bishops to censure Heydon's writers: like Luther, they said, 'they hold bishops in honour and condemn Episcopal rule'. He tried to smooth the waters by asking lay people and priests to tell him what they wanted; but he would not countenance disagreement with his policy.

People loved Polding; so his vicar general, Henry Gregory, became the target of dissent. This was unfair, no doubt, but

young Gregory was an unpopular figure. Already monks had left the monastery rather than serve under him. Marist Father Victor Poupinel wrote that he was 'odd, lacking in good sense, lacking judgement, leading the Archbishop'.

When Polding appointed a Protestant doctor to the board of the Catholic orphanage, the laity took it as an insult to themselves. Was no lay Catholic deemed suitable? 'Treason' headlined the *Freeman*, as it called on the clergy to consult over the deficiencies of diocesan leadership.

For their part, the laity packed out a protest meeting organised by Heydon. They called on Rome to provide new leadership; in the meantime, they would run the diocese themselves. Polding's response was to threaten them with excommunication. Heydon asked Father Poupinel's advice; and the next number of the *Freeman* carried his submission with a notice that he would appeal to the Holy See.

With complaints piling up, Rome sought advice from the English Benedictine Bishop W. B. Ullathorne, Polding's Vicar General in earlier days. His secret report was blunt: sack Gregory; and if that fails, sack the archbishop. So Gregory was sent home to England, never to return. Close to a crack-up, Polding blamed Heydon, calling him an infidel, a disciple of Voltaire, a Catholic in name only, who would need to do centuries of penance before he was pardoned.

J. K. Heydon survived the abuse. He sold the *Freeman* and settled to a tranquil life, broken by occasional public defences of his religion. Years later, at a parish dinner, he moved the toast to Archbishop Polding. 'He influenced his children', said a descendant, 'to strong Catholic loyalties', and certainly successive generations of the Heydon family became a creative force in the church. It just goes to show that even the saintliest bishop can sometimes be wrong.

Building for generations

WILLIAM WILKINSON WARDELL

St Patrick's Cathedral, Melbourne, is the most elegant cathedral in Australia—few would quarrel with that judgment. Before today's cathedral was built, two attempts to raise a church there had failed. These proved to be happy failures because just when church authorities were ready to make a third attempt, in 1858, William Wilkinson Wardell stepped ashore in Melbourne. He was the first Fellow of the Royal Institute of British Architects to come to Australia and authorities immediately engaged him for their cathedral. For the rest of his life he would labour over what became his masterpiece.

A Londoner, Wardell had spent a couple of years at sea as a boy. Then he became a railway surveyor, a job which took him all over Britain. This allowed him opportunities to sketch and measure ancient buildings; and so he became an architect. His mentor was A. W. Pugin, leader of the Gothic Revival

movement. Wardell was also reading John Henry Newman's Anglican writings which, combined with his love of old church buildings, led him to become a Catholic at the age of twenty. His family motto had been 'Think ye out the truth'. This he changed to 'I have found that which I sought'.

The new convert mixed in the circle of the Earl of Shrewsbury, an art patron who found him church commissions. Unlike Pugin, who concentrated on interior detail sometimes to the detriment of external finish, Wardell made his churches balanced architectural statements. He had trained as an engineer and this gave him an unusual command of the building process from drawing board to completion. He designed some thirty Catholic churches before tuberculosis drove him to emigrate to Melbourne with his wife Lucy Ann and the first of their 11 children.

In architectural circles his reputation was assured and he brought with him warm recommendations. Within months of his arrival he had won by competition the post of inspecting clerk of works and chief architect in the Department of Works and Buildings. Typically, the *Age* saw this as a Catholic plot, although the two chief 'plotters', John O'Shanassy and Charles Gavin Duffy, were in fact rivals. Such antagonism would trouble Wardell's 19 years of public service in Victoria.

His government post allowed him the right of private practice but not of on-site supervision of his buildings. To meet this difficulty, he brought a friend from England and made his designs plain and easy to follow.

Thus was he able to accept a commission to build a Catholic college at the new University of Sydney. Within a year, disputes about fees would bring his resignation. Nevertheless, St John's College at Sydney University is today substantially Wardell's. In a letter to the college fellows he urged them to remember that they were building for generations yet to come:

'What you do now do well—even if the funds at your immediate disposal require it to be less in quantity than your generosity intended'. In fact, funds ran out before the college tower was complete and it was finished short—a visual reminder of the architect's sage advice.

Archbishop Polding liked Wardell's plans for St John's College and asked him to design a new cathedral for Sydney. Thus St Mary's Cathedral joins St Patrick's and the 18 parish churches he designed in Victoria as expressions of the architect's faith. His genius was to adapt English Gothic Revival styles to Australian conditions. So, in Wardell churches—St Mary's, East St Kilda, is the best example—the hot, bright antipodean light is kept out, yet the interiors glow with warmth and serenity. In St Mary's Cathedral the ratio of stone to window glass is greater than in Chartres Cathedral. Yet the Sydney cathedral seems lighter than Chartres, its interior sandstone better able to be appreciated.

More glass meant more expense, too; and Wardell had to think of that. Already there was a saying in church circles, 'If you want to be ruined, put yourself in Wardell's hands'. People may have got the idea that he was expensive because he personally attended to every detail of his churches. This extended even to designing the pews, which he deliberately made severe because he thought church pews should not be too comfortable. Still, the severity of the pews may be a small price to pay for the glory of Wardell's architecture. Those who seek his monument have only to look around them.

From a far land
for a fruitful end

DR HENRY BACKHAUS

NOT ALL THE FOUNDERS OF CATHOLICISM IN AUSTRALIA were Irish.
From the earliest days, the sons and daughters of many lands
and many Catholic spiritual traditions brought their faith to
these shores.

An example is Dr Henry Backhaus, the priest who minis-
tered to Bendigo until the establishment of the modern
diocese of Sandhurst there. Dr Backhaus was a tall, square
but ascetic German with auburn shoulder-length hair who
spoke a heavily accented English. For the best part of 30 years
he served the people of Bendigo, baptising 10,000 of them in
that time.

His coming to Bendigo was almost an after-thought. Growing up in Paderborn, he imbibed the profound faith of that
city, which stretched back to the Dark Ages. After a year at
university, he volunteered to become a missionary and was
sent to Propaganda Fide College in Rome, the international
seminary for the missions. There he took a doctorate in

divinity and was ordained priest. A fortnight later he was on his way to Calcutta. He served as a military chaplain and brought out from Ireland a dozen young Loreto nuns to found the convent from which Mother Teresa would emerge.

Ten years in India left him with a liver complaint and sent him south of the equator towards a healthier climate. He came to Archbishop Polding's Sydney, where his musicianship is still honored by the cathedral choir, Australia's oldest church choir. There he heard that the Bishop of Adelaide needed a German-speaking priest to serve South Australia's German Catholics. So he went there and remained for four years. But times were bad and the bishop had to ask his German priest to look for work elsewhere.

Thus Dr Backhaus came to Melbourne. Within weeks he was at Bendigo, the first priest for Catholics on the goldfields. He said Mass beneath a canvas covering with his congregation under the sky. His pulpit was a tree-stump and for a collection plate he used his top hat, which the diggers filled with gold. When it was time for Mass someone hoisted a flag up on a sapling; it was lowered as Mass began and raised again at the consecration. This was frontier religion, but Dr Backhaus made sure it was not slipshod. His baptismal registers, kept as impeccably as those in any European chancery, with beautiful cursive handwriting, are testimony to his passion for good order.

The Catholic priest quickly became part of the goldfields community. In South Australia electors had petitioned him to represent them in the Legislative Council. He refused their request, but not because he wanted no part in the new society. Indeed, he had already taken the oath of allegiance, thus becoming an Australian citizen. In Bendigo he became a founding director of the local hospital and the savings bank. He supported moves to set up a mechanics' institute for adult educa-

tion. When a newspaper criticised his involvement in the secular sphere, he replied, 'I have tried to do my duty as a citizen'.

His influence could be decisive in preventing the volatile diggers from boiling over into violence. On the diggings, Chinese were targets of racist taunts and threats. Dr Backhaus spoke of the splendour of Chinese civilisation and the need for reason to curb passion. To protect the Chinese, he made jokes about himself: If the British diggers started to exterminate foreigners, would they in time come to Germans such as himself?

There was no danger of that. The people loved him and, as proof, they loaded him with gold. They knew he wasn't spending their money on himself; he led a floor-hard life, with frugal bush tucker in a cramped and cheerless presbytery. He used the money to buy land for future church purposes. Dr Backhaus had an eye for the way future Bendigo streets would run, for the direction development would take. Someone called him 'Reverend Corner Allotments' and the name stuck.

He was 70 when he died in 1882. On his deathbed he made considerable disbursements. His housekeeper was given a cheque for £16,000 to distribute to various charities. His seaside residence was meant to become an old priests' home. Already, Propaganda Fide College had been deeded hundreds of acres of Victorian farm lands for seminarians' bursaries. There were still thousands of acres in his name as well as many town allotments.

The income from these went to the church in Bendigo. In an astute move, he ensured that the estate would not be broken up soon after his death and that the money would remain in the diocese. The people of Bendigo had enriched him but he had always seen himself as their steward. That is why the diocese of Sandhurst today has so many fine Catholic buildings, crowned by its impressive cathedral. The faithful stewardship of a good German priest did all this.

Scattering the faith

Fr DUNCAN MCNAB

THESE DAYS, KITH AND KIN AND DISTANT COUSINS of Mary MacKillop are proliferating. One of the pleasant consequences of being named a saint is that hundreds of people claim to be related to you. Mary MacKillop herself was generous in her claims of kinship. It was a Celtic trait.

One whom she was proud to call her cousin was Father Duncan McNab, the Scots priest who worked for Aborigines in the nineteenth century. Ordained in 1845, he spent the first twenty years of his priesthood in Scottish parishes where many of his people were Irish labourers in retreat from the aftermath of the Great Famine. The young priest dreamed of a mission to Australian Aborigines but his bishop was reluctant to let him go.

By the time he did get away, his parents were so old that they depended totally on their priest son. So he took up parish duties again in Victorian country towns. Related to the MacKillops on the father's side, he made contact with the

family, who became his friends. The year after his arrival, McNab was called to the deathbed of Alexander MacKillop, Mary's father.

He did not give up his dream of working for Aborigines and after a few years applied to join the Benedictines at New Norcia in Western Australia, a famous centre for this work. Was he too old? In any case, his application was refused. At last, when he was 55 years old, he received permission to start a personal mission in north Queensland.

Like other priests in this field he was, in the phrase of the scholar Eugene Stockton, a maverick. Typically, says Stockton, such missionaries work on their own, or with the help of those to whom they minister. Their methods are unorthodox. They are ready to baptise, for instance, after very little instruction, trusting in the Holy Spirit to confirm their work. With minimal help from the institutional church, they are sustained by zeal amounting to a passion. Yet their memory survives long after they have died, as does the faith they scattered so randomly.

Duncan McNab is a fine example. In north Queensland he moved among the tribes, trying to learn some of their languages. He told simple stories from the Bible, baptised those who would accept the sacrament and distributed little crosses to his converts. In his diary he wrote, 'all the blacks told me that they and all to the northward had believed in the existence of God before any whites came among them'.

If Aborigines were to survive, they had to have land. Supporting Aboriginal applications for land grants, McNab wrote to the Queensland Minister of Lands that they had the best rights to it since it was 'their own country which they had always occupied and used and never renounced or alienated'. This is an early expression of what we call today the land rights case.

But McNab was unhappy in Queensland. The climate broke his health and both the bishop and the government disapproved of his work for justice. So the priest left and sailed for Europe, where he asked Pope Leo XIII to persuade a religious order to take up the Aboriginal cause in Australia. In time, his petition led to the Jesuits sending their men to the Northern Territory.

Next, McNab found his way to Western Australia, where he became chaplain to the Aboriginal prison on Rottnest Island. This taught him about the complexities of tribes and languages in the west. Now in his sixties, he decided to go north, to the rim of settled land in the Kimberleys.

He found himself among the Bard people, who appointed a minder, known as Knife, to look after him. When he had stores, the Bard people took from them, in Aboriginal sharing fashion. They liked old Father Macanab, as they called him, and enjoyed singing hymns with him, but they were uninterested in the farm he tried to start.

By now, another priest had joined him at the mission. But while McNab was away from base, this priest went down with malaria and was invalided back to Perth. In the absence of both priests the mission buildings went up in flames. McNab was too old and sick to start again. He left, accompanied on his last ride by the faithful Knife, to spend his final years with the Melbourne Jesuits. The Aborigines never forgot him and today justice workers salute this land rights pioneer.

A talent for friendship

WILLIAM HENRY ARCHER

WILLIAM HENRY ARCHER WAS A VICTORIAN WORTHY who would have been called in old-fashioned books of church history a 'Prominent Catholic Layman'. Born in London, he came to Melbourne in 1852 to improve his fortunes and was engaged by the government to set up a system for registering births, deaths and marriages. Within a few years he became the registrar-general. His collections of statistics are a valuable source for the history of Victoria.

In London Archer had become a Catholic; his enthusiasm for the church led him to work for Catholic friendly societies and insurance groups. The young immigrant soon became a valued member of the Melbourne Catholic community, adviser to Bishop Goold and a friend of John O'Shanassy, the first Catholic premier of a British territory since the Reformation. His only surviving child (of five), a daughter, would marry the son of another Catholic premier, Sir Charles Gavan Duffy.

Archer represented the Catholic interest on successive schools boards until the phasing out of state aid to church

schools in 1872. Thereafter he continued to campaign for the reintroduction of state aid through publications, a laymen's lobby group and his minority report to a royal commission on education. He organised regular evening meetings of Catholics to discuss cultural and scientific topics. Typically, when John Henry Newman became a cardinal, Archer promoted an Australian gift of silver plate for him. His work for the church was recognised by his appointment as a papal knight.

Bishop Goold went to Archer for advice. In a famous episode the bishop came under heavy criticism from a group of the laity who alleged financial mismanagement. Archer read their memorial and annotated it savagely. Then he wrote a counter memorial supporting the bishop and had prominent laymen sign it. To the bishop he suggested that a few Christian Brothers and Jesuits in the diocese would help the church, as would the appointment of laity to financial committees. But Bishop Goold was not ready for such advice then.

Archer's close association with Catholic interests penalised him in public life, especially after his dismissal as registrar-general on 'Black Wednesday' 1878, when the government sacked many public servants. His income reduced, he filled his time with books, art and science. One of the things which sustained him was his friendship with that remarkable priest, Father Julian Tenison Woods. Father Julian's letters to him over 25 years have been published by Sister Anne Player of North Goulburn (NSW).

The letters show the priest's talent for friendship and, because they are private letters, they reveal aspects of his personality not commonly known. He is playful and skittish, almost boyish even. When Archer becomes a papal knight, for example, Julian insists on calling him Sir William, although he does not do so in public. Their shared interest in science is a bond between them, Julian using Archer as an agent

to obtain a microscope and to promote his own writings.

In passing, the letters give precious details of Julian's life as a priest. As parish priest of Penola in South Australia, he spent many days on his horse and many nights camping with the fleas in shepherds' huts. Later, he writes of giving parish missions in northern Queensland, where he was laid up by fever. The next letter in the collection speaks of missions in Tasmania, where surviving records of Holy Communions at his missions attest the success of his preaching. Thence to Sydney, in time to observe the dying Archbishop Polding ('The old Archbishop is a complete wreck: fast slipping away') and to be befriended by the new man, Archbishop Vaughan.

The country parishes of NSW keep him busy with missions, the days filled with hearing confessions and preaching morning and night. Soon, however, Julian's career as a missioner would be over. The arrival of religious orders made his sort of freelance preaching obsolete. As well, clerical jealousy stood in his way, although he tried to keep a low profile by avoiding meetings of the clergy.

So when a friend invited him to make a scientific expedition through South East Asia, he accepted the invitation. His letters to Archer now frequently mention his poor health— testimony that the hard-riding years of his priestly youth had taxed him. By the time he got back to Sydney, he was finished. He could not walk more than 50 yards and had lost the use of his hands, so that he could do no more science.

Nor did the church have any further use for him. The dawning recognition of that had driven him to South East Asia. In one completely frank letter to Archer he shared with his friend his weariness at the 'unkindness, hard usage, envy and bitterness' which had become his lot in the Australian church.

And so he died, aged 57. His letters, preserved by W. H. Archer, are a sad memorial to their friendship.

A dream that failed

FR DONALD MACKILLOP

THE NORTHERN TERRITORY JESUIT MISSION in the final decades of the 19th century deserves to be remembered because it provided signposts to the future.

At the urging of Roman authorities and with the promise of support from Australian bishops, Jesuits arrived from the south in 1882. Before setting out, they had studied Aboriginal culture and language as best they could. This sensitivity towards the people they lived among was to remain a feature of the Jesuits and their lasting contribution to missionary understanding. They were open to other belief systems and refused to condemn them out of hand as 'heathenism'. Far from rejecting Aboriginal culture, they believed, Christianity should build on the many worthwhile elements found there. Humility and respect for others were essential virtues.

The Jesuits became adepts of local languages, working hard to achieve fluency. A catechism they wrote was revised twenty times to ensure that it captured the complex grammar

of those it would teach. Hymns and secular songs, often set to popular tunes of the time, were another achievement. Astonishingly, the Mass was translated into a local language and set to Haydn's music. They collected valuable lexicographical evidence of what were still living languages. Decades later, an Aboriginal ancient remembered them fondly: 'The Jesuits were very good. They never beat us'.

There are, of course, two sides to that compliment. The down side is the recognition that if the Jesuits were not cruel, their fellow whites certainly were. In the frontier territory gun law ruled. Aborigines were forced off their land, pillaged, diseased and killed. The women were taken into sexual slavery. Hunters and gathers were reduced to begging in the streets. The prevailing philosophy, Darwinism, regarded Aborigines as an inferior race who were destined to die out—and the sooner the better.

The Jesuit plan was to settle Aborigines on the land and make them into farmers who lived in family homes or communal dormitories. They aimed to establish farming communes which in time (several generations, perhaps) would become Christian. The model for this was the Jesuit 'Reductions' in Paraguay in the 17th and 18th centuries. But this would not work in Australia, where Aborigines preferred to sleep outside around a fire or under bark, getting their food from daily hunting and fishing. And the vices of other newcomers proved very seductive, whether it was Europeans' liquor or the opium available from the numerous Chinese.

At first the Jesuits had settled in what is now a suburb of Darwin. After a few years, in search of solitude, they moved 250 kilometres away to the Daly River and pitched their tents by the riverside at a spot called Uniya. The river water tasted to them of crocodiles and the land was stony and inhos-

tages as a bonus, since

this would keep other whites away from the local tribes. So they planted rice and vegetable gardens and tried to interest Aborigines in agriculture. But each year the Wet wiped out their crops. Disease was constant: malaria, pneumonia, eye trouble, fevers, diarrhoea.

Facing starvation, they appealed to Australian Catholics for help. Their superior, Father Donald MacKillop, brother of the saintly Mary MacKillop, went south on a fund-raising expedition. He took two young Aboriginal men with him, dressed as Europeans, and his expedition brought in enough cash to keep them going for a few more years. More importantly, he used his time down south to alert his fellow Australians to the dangers of Darwinian thinking and the human cost of white settlement.

As human beings, he argued, Aborigines were the equal of whites. Fashionable ideas about British 'superiority' to black culture should not be allowed to cover up what was plainly murder. It was the strong versus the weak, rifles against spears; but might was not right. One day, perhaps centuries hence, the invaders could themselves suffer invasion. In the meantime the Jesuit mission must be helped to save the remnant from destruction.

Great people live by their dreams, which may turn into nightmares. Archbishop Polding had dreamt of missionising Australia with wandering Benedictine monks, just as monks had missioned Europe in the Dark Ages. But other times needed other plans. Similarly, Donald MacKillop and the Uniya Jesuits dreamt of recreating the Reductions of Paraguay in the Northern Territory. That failed too. Nevertheless, their dream still has much to teach us.

Mary's friends and benefactors

JOANNA BARR SMITH

WHEN POPE JOHN PAUL II CAME TO AUSTRALIA in January 1995, he visited the grave of Mary MacKillop in her memorial chapel at North Sydney. Following his usual custom, he knelt and kissed the marble slab over the grave. In a strange way, his kiss was an ecumenical gesture. For the marble slab was paid for by a remarkable Presbyterian lady, Joanna Barr Smith.

A daughter of the wealthy Elder family, she had married Robert Barr Smith in 1856, when she was 21. They were to have thirteen children, six of whom died in infancy. Born in Scotland, the son of a Presbyterian minister, Robert went into business with Thomas Elder, his wife's unmarried brother. They were the sole partners of Elder Smith & Co., a pastoral company which held extensive leases in South Australia, Queensland, New South Wales and Victoria, as well as copper mines and shipping companies.

By the end of the century people said Robert Barr Smith was the wealthiest man in Australia. The family lived well and were famous party-givers. They owned vast houses in Adelaide and, for holidays, in the Adelaide hills. These houses were sumptuously decorated and appointed—over 800 items of table glass, for instance, were once ordered from London.

Modern South Australians recall the Barr Smith homes with delight because they were furnished principally by Morris & Co., London. William Morris used natural dyes and his tapestries and wallpapers had deep lasting colours and rich intricate designs. In the main rooms of the Barr Smith homes, golden wallpaper set off an extravagance of curtains, upholstery and embroideries, with bibelots and ceramics crowding every flat surface. Happily, the Art Gallery of South Australia has acquired much of this rare Morris collection, which surviving photographs show in its original opulent settings.

Robert and Joanna Barr Smith were open-handed with their money. Their benefactions made life in South Australia more attractive—pictures for the art gallery, an observatory, a lifeboat, ambulances and so much money to the university that the library was named the Barr Smith Library. Although themselves Presbyterians, they gave £10,000 towards the completion of the spires of the Anglican cathedral and another £2000 to help establish a second Anglican diocese in South Australia.

And they were benefactors of Mary MacKillop. We do not know how Mary and Joanna met but their Scots blood was one certain link. We know that it was in the early days of the Josephites because Joanna once wrote to Mary about those days, regretting the passing of the spirit of simplicity so noticeable to her then.

Throughout the years they kept in touch, with Mary sending birthday cards and occasional letters. When her Jesuit brother, Donald, passed through Adelaide from his Daly River mission, she made sure he contacted her friend for a donation. Joanna once insisted that she be allowed to pay for a sleeper on the train to Melbourne, so that Mary might have some rest.

Then, when the main Adelaide convent at Kensington needed extensions, Mary turned again to her old friend. She was not disappointed, for the Barr Smiths gave her the money she wanted. Often she reminded her sisters of the liberality of these non-Catholic friends. Privately she hoped that some Catholic magnifico might match their generosity.

Two years before she died, Mary sent Joanna a meditation she had written on the comfort and support Jesus can give to the downhearted. 'Ah, dearest Mother Mary', wrote back her friend, 'we are all weary and disappointed when we get old. Well for us if we have some hope of life beyond this. I like your little paper so much. It speaks to my heart and I envy you the life you have been able to live.'

When Mary MacKillop left Adelaide for the last time, Joanna Barr Smith had been at the railway station with her husband to farewell her. Her final letter to Mary is a noble testament to their friendship. 'Oh, my dear friend, I wish I could see you again or hear your voice', she wrote. 'Living or dying, my beloved friend, I am ever the same to you and am proud to look back on nearly forty years of unbroken friendship.'

Mary MacKillop's tomb in the North Sydney chapel was a last gift from Joanna Barr Smith. Although her remains have been relocated in the chapel, the marble slab is still there, testimony to the long friendship between a Catholic saint and her Presbyterian benefactor.

A candidate for canonisation

CHARLES GORDON O'NEILL

HIS REMAINS LIE IN A PAUPER'S GRAVE in Rookwood cemetery, yet some people continue to hope that one day he will be canonised. He is Charles Gordon O'Neill, a Glasgow Irishman who came to Australia in 1881 and founded the Society of St Vincent de Paul here.

During the goldrush years there had been fitful appearances of the St Vincent de Paul Society which soon disappeared, its work taken over by religious orders. It was O'Neill's tenacity and devotion which ensured that this best-loved Catholic lay society became established and survived in Australia.

The son of an emigrant Irish publican, O'Neill had graduated as a civil engineer in Scotland. He joined the St Vincent de Paul and within a decade became local president, as well as a member of the international council in Paris.

Then he went out to New Zealand to work as a surveyor and provincial engineer. Train lines, the Wellington tramway system, the water supply, bridge-building, town planning—these were some of his projects. For ten years he was a Member of Parliament too.

In New Zealand he became an active St Vincent de Paul man again, setting up the Wellington conference, the first New Zealand conference to be recognised by Paris. Writing to him, the President-General suggested that he might be able to establish the society in Sydney and other Australian cities with the help of the French Marist Fathers there.

So O'Neill moved to Sydney and soon made contact with the Marists at Church Hill in the central business district. A conference was set up there in July 1881 and by the end of that year there were four conferences in the inner city. By 1890 there were twenty conferences in Sydney.

Historians agree that this solid growth owed much to O'Neill's enthusiasm and encouragement. While he continued his work as an engineer—he planned a tunnel under Sydney Harbour a century before it became a reality—the society absorbed his attention. He spent his time going from parish to parish enlisting members, raising support and putting conferences in touch with each other. He insisted that members stick to the St Vincent de Paul rule that poverty was the only claim the poor needed to enlist their help. 'We are not to enquire to what party or sect they belong.'

Weekly meetings followed the pattern laid down in the 1830s by their French founder, Frederick Ozanam: a short prayer, a spiritual reflection, assessment of local needs and what to do about them, a secret collection and the final prayer. Members went out in pairs to visit needy families week by week, although the sick might be visited daily.

To raise funds, O'Neill's society proved themselves inventive. Dances, slide shows and concerts were regular events to augment the parish poor boxes. One St Patrick's Day they sold artificial shamrock buttonholes. They showed flexibility also in meeting special needs. To develop thrifty habits they founded 'penny banks' for children; soon adults too were using these peoples' banks, prototypes of 20th century credit unions.

Charles O'Neill's St Vincent de Paul manual has survived, a precious piece of historical evidence, for he wrote in it the date each conference was formed. Much more precious, however, are the clippings and quotations he filed there. They provide a window into the soul of this splendid Catholic layman.

One of them is a quotation from St Vincent de Paul himself: 'Those who love the poor in life shall have no fear in death'. Another quotes some words of Ozanam: 'This dear Society is also my family. Next to God it was the means of preserving my faith after I left my good and pious parents. I love it therefore with all my heart'.

Yet in 1891 he resigned as president, apparently to protect the society from any adverse publicity flowing from an impending court case. An inattentive director of a bank which failed, he was charged but acquitted of any misconduct. The acquittal cleared his name; however he did not return to the presidency of the society he loved, although his commitment did not waver.

O'Neill never married, and shared poor lodgings with his bachelor brother in The Rocks. In his last illness in 1900 he was attended by the legendary Marist Father Piquet, first chaplain to the society. Sixty years later his remains were reinterred in the St Vincent de Paul burial plot for the destitute, which he now shares with those he served so well. 'He lived a life of unobtrusive but resplendent and enduring charity', said the historian Bede Nairn, 'and is at least as good a candidate for canonisation as Caroline Chisholm.'

Our valiant
women

KATE DWYER, ANNIE &
BELLE GOLDING

FOREMOTHERS, HISTORIAN SOPHIE MCGRATH HAS CALLED THEM. And so indeed they are—the valiant women of an earlier age who established a tradition and became role models for later generations. Such were Kate Dwyer and her sisters Annie and Belle Golding, whose long, active lives deserve to be remembered.

The three sisters were schoolteachers, an occupation filled by many Catholic women in the 19th century. After a few years teaching, Kate married a fellow teacher who then became headmaster of the Broken Hill public school. It was a time of bad drought as well as a lengthy strike, when the sufferings of working people and their families radicalised the headmaster's wife.

Teaching also radicalised the other sisters. Annie taught at many schools in Sydney and the bush, including a stint at an asylum for destitute children. She joined the teachers' trade union and soon became a union official. Several times she was passed over for promotions which she thought she had deserved.

Belle also started life as a teacher but she soon became a public servant charged with inspecting working conditions of women. Her reports reveal her deep concern for justice for women at work. Less politically active than her sisters, she backed their public statements and speeches with detailed research.

Early in their careers the three sisters joined together to win women the vote. As suffragettes, they were younger contemporaries of the formidable feminist Rose Scott and for a time her co-workers. While Rose was promoting feminism in the fashionable drawing rooms of Woollahra, the Golding sisters worked the stonier ground of Newtown and Annandale.

They found a supporter in Cardinal Moran, who arranged for Annie to speak at his national Catholic conferences. Her first address, in 1904, was at a time when both Victoria and Queensland still denied women the vote. She argued that female franchise would promote prosperity, peace and freedom.

Her second address, at the 1909 conference, was more down-to-earth, drawing on Belle's research. Her opening sentences asserted that a nation would be judged on its treatment of women. With detailed evidence from several industries, she called for equal pay for women. She also wanted to see a Professor of Domestic Science at Sydney University.

This curious proposal was not forgotten, for in the next decade her sister Kate was appointed to the university senate, where she lobbied for a chair of domestic science. Kate's senate appointment is an index of her standing in the wider community.

Her interest in female suffrage had led her into further political involvement. She joined the Labor Party, as did her sisters, and organised campaigns for the right of women to join professions and to have fair shares of matrimonial property. Women were always the centre of her attention. She organised a union for women who worked part time or at home.

She gave evidence to royal commissions on housing and on female and juvenile workers. She sat on a royal commission into food and on wages boards and conciliation committees. She hoped to enter parliament but never made it, although she was a member of the committee directing the 'No' campaign against wartime conscription.

The Golding sisters' agenda covered many fields: women's equality before the law, equal pay, child welfare, women's hospitals, Aboriginal children, cheap housing, better schools, factory conditions and the appointment of women as police officers and justices of the peace. It was a matter of pride to them when Kate was made a justice of the peace in 1921, one of the first female JPs in NSW.

It is worth noting that their citizenly contributions in every field were practical, knowledgeable and pragmatic rather than utopian. No mere dreamers, they got out and brought pressure to bear on the men who were framing the legislation which would affect women's lives. They believed in changing society by gradual pressure. And they never let up.

Each of them, according to biographers, was a practising, even devout, Catholic, They are examples to later generations of the Catholic social justice option expressed in practical terms. Modern Catholic women, whether they call themselves feminists or not and whatever their personal politics, will recognise the authenticity of the Golding sisters. They were true foremothers.

The ties that divide

THOMAS HENRY FIASCHI

THE MOST POPULAR STATUE IN SYDNEY sits outside Sydney Hospital in Macquarie Street. A great hairy boar, a replica of Florence's 'Il Porcellino', its snout is patted and stroked by countless visitors who also put money into its collection box. The boar is a monument to a Sydney Hospital surgeon, Thomas Henry Fiaschi, who died in 1927

Born in Florence to a mathematics professor and his English wife, Fiaschi studied medicine before coming to Australia at the age of 21. He tried his luck on the Queensland goldfields and then became house surgeon at St Vincent's Hospital, Sydney. He returned to Italy to take medical and surgical degrees and came back to Sydney, where he went into general practice.

His real interest was surgery. Service in both the Australian and Italian medical corps extended his experience. He served as a doctor in the Abyssinian war, the South African war and World War I and was decorated by both countries, rising to the rank of brigadier-general.

At Sydney Hospital, where he was an honorary surgeon, Fiaschi was known as a good teacher. Abrupt and quick-tempered when he detected slipshod medical procedures, he was nevertheless admired for never bearing a grudge. His sense of humour made him popular and in time he became one of the hospital characters about whom many stories were told. He was conscientious in keeping up with his medical reading and in publishing professional papers.

There were other sides to Dr Fiaschi. He was a pioneer of Australian wines, with vineyards on the Hawkesbury and out west at Mudgee. From the island of Elba he brought cuttings of the vines that made Napoleon's favourite aleatico, a roseate dessert wine with a fine bouquet. These cuttings struck at Mudgee, where the vines still produce an occasional vintage much prized by wine lovers.

Dr Fiaschi was well known in Sydney's cultural life. He founded the Dante Alighieri Society to bring European perspectives to a narrowly British city. His friends subscribed to a portrait of him by the reigning master, Antonio Dattilo-Rubbo, and gave him a book of their autographs illuminated by Hardy Wilson. Tall and dignified, with piercing good looks, he was a distinctive figure in Macquarie Street.

In 1910 tragedy struck. His son Carlo Ferruchio, also a doctor, was arraigned on a charge of doing an abortion. For lack of evidence Carlo was acquitted but the experience preyed on his mind and drove him to drink until, after a week or so, he killed himself. He was buried in the Anglican section of Waverley cemetery, where today a broken column over his grave recalls his interrupted life.

A few days after the funeral his father received another blow. Thirty-five years earlier at St Vincent's Hospital he had fallen in love with one of the nuns, Catherine Reynolds, known in religion as Sister Mary Regis. They ran away together and got married, which incurred excommunication from the church. That was a long time ago and in the meantime Dr Fiaschi had become a respected Macquarie Street surgeon.

A few months before the suicide, the Mother Rectress of St Vincent's had called on the surgeon and his wife and invited him to send patients to the private wing of the hospital. On the part of the nuns it was a conciliatory gesture, a kindly overreaching of the strictures of canon law, and Dr Fiaschi was happy to send some of his Catholic patients to the private hospital.

The scandal of the suicide excited gossips and soon all Sydney knew the details of the Fiaschi's marriage. Then Dr Fiaschi received a shocking letter from the Superior General of the nuns. In two sentences she asked him to sever his connection with the private hospital, giving as her reason 'unrest and dissatisfaction' among the nuns over the current gossip. His reply was a dignified but protesting compliance with her will.

Then he sent the correspondence to the press. The letters to the editor which followed are a case study in misunderstanding between Catholics and Protestants. It did not help that a play about the Massacre of St Bartholomew's Eve was currently running in Sydney, reviving memories of the pogrom against Protestants in sixteenth century France.

Beside those highwater marks of Australian sectarian conflict, the O'Haran case, the Mother Liguori case and the Jerger case, the Fiaschi case is small beer. Still, whenever a priest walks past that memorial in Macquarie Street, the Florentine boar seems to growl at him.

Fired by love's urgent longings

EILEEN O'CONNOR

SHE WAS ALWAYS TINY. Although she lived to be 28, she never grew to be more than a bit above a metre. At the age of three she had fallen from a pram and broken her back. Badly diagnosed, the accident led to permanent curvature of the spine. All her life she seems to have been in pain. Sometimes she would be comatose from pain; at other times she would lose consciousness altogether. Operations to correct the spinal curvature added to her sufferings.

Nevertheless, Eileen O'Connor became a heroic figure in the story of Australian Catholics. She founded a religious society, Our Lady's Nurses for the Poor, also known as the Brown Sisters because they wore brown cloaks (for St Joseph) over their nurses' white. For three-quarters of a century they have nursed the sick poor in their own homes. In all that time they have drawn inspiration from the sickly saint they still call 'the Little Mother'.

Some years after her accident, Eileen's family brought her

from Melbourne to Sydney, where her father had found employment as an accountant. When she was 19, however, her father died. There was no widow's pension then so, with the help of the local clergy, her mother rented a house in seaside Coogee and took in lodgers.

Thus Eileen came to know the parish priest, a young Australian Missionary of the Sacred Heart (MSC), Fr Ted McGrath. He brought her Holy Communion and shared her confidences. Bedridden as she was most of the time, she offered her suffering as a share in the parish priest's apostolate. She wanted, she told him, 'to be a nun as far as I can'.

Together they developed plans for a new religious institute to care for poor people disabled by sickness. Instead of taking them into hospitals, institute members would go out to the poor in their own homes and care for them there. Always in the background at home would be Eileen O'Connor, sharing in the work by her offered sufferings and prayer.

A beginning was made in 1913, but the work moved slowly. It took 18 months for the first seven recruits to gather. The first of them, Cissie McLaughlin, had been thinking of becoming a nun but was put off the idea because in those days most religious sisters taught in schools and Cissie did not want to be a teacher. She went out to Coogee and talked things over with Eileen. Afterwards, waiting at the tram stop, she had an overpowering impulse to join in the new work. It was, she said, as if Eileen had sent an angel after her to convince her.

The Brown Sisters lived in their own home, thanks to the munificence of Fr Edward Gell, a Sydney parish priest, and his sister Frances, who used their family money for religious causes. Frances Gell gave her cheque to Fr McGrath, while her brother gave his to Eileen; so the title deeds listed the two founders as joint owners. Therein lay future trouble.

Soon afterwards, a visiting MSC potentate turned a cold

eye on Fr McGrath's involvement and ordered him to restrict his contacts with the nurses. The superior was a canon lawyer, so when he discovered that the priest's name was on those title deeds he reacted sharply, ordering him to remove his name. In Fr McGrath's eyes to do so would display a lack of confidence in the nurses. He resisted the command.

Sent to Tasmania, he returned to argue his case. Eileen, who had recently experienced a mysterious partial recovery of the use of her legs, followed him south, urging him to remain true to his MSC vocation. Then, however, Fr Gell took a party on a Pacific cruise, including the two founders. When they returned, Fr McGrath was informed that he was expelled from the MSC congregation for public scandal. The implication of this was obvious; and Eileen's lawyer wanted her (and her personal nurse) to sue for defamation.

Instead, she urged her friend to go to Rome to clear his name. She would go with him because, aware of her deformity, she argued that people could see with their own eyes that it would be impossible for her to be what the dismissal alleged.

In time, the priest was declared innocent. The English Cardinal Gasquet told him, 'They have treated you not only unjustly but shamefully and unnaturally'. He remained in exile, returning to live in Australia only during World War II.

In the meantime, Eileen resumed her presence at Coogee. People came to her from all over Sydney, seeking advice and consolation. Although she could walk a little, her spinal pain had not abated. To it was now added the suffering of separation from her co-founder. She died in 1921, aged 28.

Breaking free

ANNA BRENNAN

AT THE AGE OF 83, Anna Brennan went to the university to hear a lecture on nuclear fission, slipped on the steps, got pneumonia and died. Her friends thought the circumstances of her death were symbolic. This pioneering Catholic feminist died as she had lived, stretching out for deeper experience of life.

The thirteenth child of farmers, she grew up in a family circle which was intellectually stimulating and devoutly Catholic. Belonging to the Brennan family was an education in itself. At table, questions of the day were debated and the children were encouraged to use their talents while developing their social conscience.

Her brother Frank became attorney-general in the Scullin Labor government and an expert in international affairs. Another brother was a founder of the Catholic Federation, the umbrella organisation which protected Catholic interests in the early 20th century, and the first president of the Newman

Society at Melbourne University. A third brother became chief leader-writer on the *Argus*.

The Brennan brothers urged their youngest sister to use her brains and said they would support her at university. At first she enrolled in Medicine but then switched to Law. Student politics was a valuable part of her education, providing her with networks, experience and above all self-confidence that would last through her life.

She was admitted to legal practice in 1911, the first locally-born woman to be admitted to practice in Victoria. She went into partnership with her brother Frank, specialising in matrimonial cases. Throughout her life she argued for equitable divorce laws, without the kinks and collusions which demeaned litigants. During World War II, with Dame Enid Lyons, she served on a government committee to protect the rights of Australian women married to aliens. Representing the National Council of Women, she had already advised the government on the legislation needed to protect these rights.

Anna Brennan's association with the National Council of Women went back to her university days. As an activist in the women's student union she was led to the National Council, where she represented the students. When the Lyceum Club, a women's literary and social forum, was founded she became one of its first members. She would serve as trustee, legal adviser and president. She was president also of the Legal Women's Association.

Such communal service was an aspect of her outgoing Catholicism. She believed that to be Christian was to use your talents serving others. In line with this, she helped found the Catholic Women's Social Guild, becoming a member of its first committee and the guild's second president. She was a frequent speaker on guild platforms and wrote for its publications.

The guild was a Catholic feminist body. It offered lay women an active role in public life, refusing to confine them to the stereotypes of the 'homemaker'. At its first general meeting Anna Brennan warned her listeners about the tyranny of housework, how it could deaden them and kill any desire to change the world. Worse—they could be trapped into seeing their nice homes as a measure of social status.

The guild tried to energise lay Catholic women into keeping a watch on social and political issues, particularly those affecting women, and to take appropriate action, either on their own or in concert with other women's organisations. Early in its life it affiliated with the National Council of Women.

Therein lay future trouble. The conscription referenda during World War I produced an explosion of sectarianism, which rallied Melbourne Catholics to demonstrate loyalty to their archbishop, Daniel Mannix. Loyalty to Archbishop Mannix, whatever the cause, became a test of Catholicity. So when the president of the National Council of Women made a speech attacking the archbishop's politics, it provoked a crisis in the guild. Pressure was mounted to disaffiliate.

Anna Brennan kept her head and tried to calm tempers. Then the archbishop let it be known that he insisted on disaffiliation. At issue was the question of who controlled the guild: the women or the archbishop. The archbishop won, and Anna Brennan resigned. For the rest of her life she maintained her support for Catholic feminism, in the St Joan's Alliance, for instance. But she never again wasted time on lay bodies controlled by the clergy.

Boxing Les
An Australian icon

LES DARCY

BOXING IS UGLY, BRUTAL AND CRUEL and no one would rank it in the upper reaches of civilisation. Yet from the time of David and Goliath individual fighters have been made into heroes by common consent of ordinary people. Historians must take the past as they find it and make what sense they can of it. So while they might think that boxing is as uncivilised as bear-baiting or cock-fighting, they cannot shut their eyes to the fame once enjoyed by pugilists.

Take Les Darcy. Born in 1895, he grew up at a time when boxing was extravagantly popular. The Sydney Stadium, built in 1908 to accommodate a world heavyweight championship fight, could seat 15,000 fans. It was said to be the biggest stadium in the world. Brisbane and Melbourne had similar venues, while fight magazines and weekly newspapers found a wide readership.

All over the country, boys were swept up in this enthusiasm, shaping up against each other in sheds, barns and cleared spaces in city lanes as they learnt the craft of boxing. In part, money was a lure; for at a time when a skilled man's wages might be three pounds a week, the main bout at Sydney Stadium was worth as much as £500 to each contestant.

Money was certainly part of the attraction for Les Darcy. His father was a rural worker of irregular employment and there were 12 children in the family. Leaving school at the age of 12, Les did odd jobs until he became an apprentice to the local blacksmith. He was already boxing, making his first money in the ring when he was 14 years old. Blacksmith's work developed his physique and gave him a famously strong neck, which made him impervious to the hardest blows.

Soon he became a regular drawcard at Sydney Stadium against American imports. In 20 months he won 22 successive fights and some good judges began to say he was the best in the world. With the prize money, he bought his parents a home in Maitland, filling it with furniture and clothes for his brothers and sisters. He did not smoke or drink but liked to race a Studebaker along country roads. To calm pre-fight nerves, he played a mouth organ.

While Les Darcy was making his name as a boxer, the world had gone to war. After Gallipoli, as war losses mounted, pressures increased for more recruitment. Les said he wanted to enlist, but he was under age and his mother would not give the necessary permission. Then the government decided to hold a referendum on conscription, three days before his 21st birthday.

The electorate said No; but the day before the referendum Les had stowed away on a ship to the USA. Stung by the loss of the referendum, government supporters took out their anger on him, labelling him a 'shirker' and a 'slacker'. In vain he protested that he only wanted four or five fights in the USA to set up his family; then he would go to Canada and enlist.

The Sydney Stadium management brought pressure on American governors, who barred Les from boxing in several states. At last a bout was scheduled for Memphis, Tennessee, but he collapsed while training and died in hospital, his Australian fiancee by his bedside. Hundreds of thousands turned out to salute the return of the dead hero to Australian soil.

In Les Darcy they recognised a finer, enlarged version of themselves. Here was someone who had developed his talents to the utmost, to provide for his mother and father and family. He faced life with a cheerful grin—that grin was famous—and took life as it came to him without gloom. For Catholics, he was a model: a daily Mass-goer, morally sound and a friend of the local priest.

Yet this paragon had been struck down, almost, some people said, as if he were a martyr. There were dark rumours that 'the Yanks poisoned Les Darcy' but that was a furphy. What killed him was heart trouble and blood poisoning from broken teeth. The humans at fault were not Americans but those ascendancy Australians who hounded him in order to punish those like him who had voted against conscription.

Like 60,000 others of that Gallipoli generation, his life was cut short and so he became a symbol of them all. He stands too for hopes unrealised, ambitions thwarted and redemption through suffering. That is why Les Darcy is still a national icon, even for those who dislike boxing.

A lonely
death

ANNIE EGAN

THE END OF WORLD WAR I saw an outbreak of Spanish influenza which soon reached the Pacific region. Soldiers returning home on troopships were particularly vulnerable. By early December 1918, 2000 deaths had been reported in New Zealand. The virus was slower to attack Australia. But by December at least 33 men had died aboard Australian transports.

The government moved swiftly to protect the continent. Principal target areas were the ports of Melbourne and Sydney, with Sydney being considered the most vulnerable. Strict quarantine rules were enforced, so that soon Sydney Harbour was crowded with ships in process of quarantine.

To care for the expanded population in quarantine, the government advertised for extra nurses. Among the first to respond was Nurse Annie Egan, a 27-year-old graduate of St Vincent's Hospital in Sydney. She had volunteered for the military nursing service and this was her first posting. A telegram ordered her to meet Nurse Williams, also a recent graduate of St Vincent's, and report immediately for duty at the Manly quarantine station.

She did not even have time to tell her parents. They were farming people from Gunnedah (NSW), where Annie had gone to the convent school. There were six children in the family, two of them nuns. The first the family heard of Annie's enlistment was an official telegram eight days after her arrival at Manly. It brought the cruel news that she had died from influenza.

Although inoculated, she had contracted the virus soon after arrival. She worked for three more days then collapsed. Thinking she might be in danger, she asked for a priest. A short time earlier there had been three priests in quarantine but they had been discharged. Now Annie's request was refused. Nurse Williams telephoned the rectress at St Vincent's, who alerted the cathedral.

Still the quarantine superintendent, Dr J. S. E. Elkington, would not relent. A secularist, he was a friend of Norman Lindsay and shared Lindsay's distaste for religion. Some priests said they were willing to go into quarantine and stay there, sleeping on the ground if necessary, but Dr Elkington still refused.

After an appeal to the government, Archbishop Kelly announced that he would present himself at the quarantine gates to bring the sacraments to the dying nurse. In vain. With four of his priests he drove to the gates but was refused entry by Elkington's command. The next day Nurse Egan died. She was buried in the little quarantine cemetery, where her grave can still be seen.

Her death in such circumstances brought on an explosion of indignation among Catholics across Australia. In dozens of parishes, meetings protested the denial of the last sacraments to the nurse. Angry speeches fuelled the sense of outrage. Bishops sent messages to the government and to individual MPs.

A solemn requiem Mass was held for Nurse Egan at the Sydney cathedral. It was an impressive occasion, the sanctuary packed with monsignori, members of religious orders and the secular clergy. The parents of the dead Nurse Egan had been brought from Gunnedah for the Mass. In the congregation were representatives of Catholic societies, politicians and legal men, nuns from St Vincent's, as well as military and civil nurses.

Archbishop Kelly preached a long sermon. He spoke, said the press, 'with great emotion and intensity of expression, that deeply moved the vast congregation'. Towards the end he got carried away and almost descended to farce, saying that he himself might have rowed into the quarantine station or scaled the wall with an eight-foot ladder. Then he remembered the dead nurse and brought the congregation to its knees reciting the *De Profundis*.

The daily press supported these Catholic protests. Support came also from leading politicians and the Chief Justice, who called the refusal of the last sacraments 'cruel and unjust'. A former Presbyterian moderator wrote to the press and an Anglican archdeacon denounced the refusal from his pulpit. Labor journalist Mary Gilmore sent a poem to the Catholic press. The government quickly capitulated, announcing that in future priests would be allowed into quarantine stations.

The lonely death of Nurse Egan—by official *diktat* unshriven, unhouseled, unaneled—is one of those episodes of history which touch a sudden nerve. As well as sympathy with the dead nurse, Catholics showed by their protests that they were willing to fight for their rights whenever necessary.

Choosing a 'necessary isolation'

Cardinal NORMAN THOMAS GILROY

Norman Thomas Gilroy was Archbishop of Sydney for 31 years and became the first Australian-born cardinal. When he retired, in 1971, the *Sydney Morning Herald* carried a long editorial lauding his stewardship, especially praising his leadership in dampening sectarianism, which elsewhere had flared up because of the Church's involvement in politics.

Away from the headlines, Cardinal Gilroy was attentive to the demands of rank and file members of the church. Obscure parishioners would write to him and he would reply in his own hand. Each Saturday he sat in the cathedral for four hours, hearing the worries and complaints of those who sought him out. On the other hand, he was hard on his priests, some of whom bore the scars of his episcopal attention all their lives. He had no personal friends, he informed a journalist before he retired. He told priests at the cathedral that being a bishop brought with it a 'necessary isolation'.

Cardinal Gilroy wasn't always like that. Starting life as a GPO messenger boy, he had advanced to being a telegraphist in the bush when World War I broke out and he volunteered for service as an assistant wireless operator. So in February 1915, having just turned 19, he sailed for Egypt and Gallipoli. He would be away for nine months—'the most valuable and educational period of my 20 years of existence'.

This comment appears on the final page of a diary he kept on board ship. It is a revealing document, a corrective to those who knew him only as an ecclesiastical iron man. Of prime value to a biographer, the diary raises teasing questions about how his personality changed. What wrought that change?

There is no sign in the diary of the 'necessary isolation' of later years. At each port of call, he goes ashore with shipmates and tours the sights. Rowed ashore in Colombo, they refuse to tip the boatmen ('they were still asking when we left the wharf') and go for a spin round town in rickshaws. They patronise a gully gully man and stop for refreshments at fashionable hotels, although the diarist complains that it is sometimes hard to get his preferred lemon squash—he was to remain a teetotaller throughout his life.

His ship was in the line at Gallipoli and his diary records details of the landing with boyish gusto. It is unreflective, surface reporting which was consonant with his youth. Years later, he was to write more reflectively of how he came to realise at Gallipoli what little control men had over their own lives. Such ruminations, if they occurred then, were not put in the diary.

After Gallipoli, his ship took him to London for three weeks of fun. He goes sight-seeing in the great city, lunching and dining in hotels. He has a suit made and buys a velour hat but dislikes the colour. Later he will have it dyed. With one of his mates he visits a Turkish bath house. Many nights he goes to a theatre or a music hall and the diary carries critical comments on the performances. In later life he would show little of such interest in human culture—more of his 'necessary isolation'.

In the parish near the docks he meets a Father Davidson, with whom he has long conversations. They go to town together, to Mass at Westminster Cathedral, where the future cardinal meets the vicar-general ('old but very clever man'). He thought the unfinished cathedral the most beautifully decorated place he had ever seen. Westminster Abbey made him think sadly of the monks who had once been there.

Nevertheless, for the young Norman Thomas Gilroy religion was not then as all-pervasive as it would become. There is a startling entry in the diary for 2 April 1915, when he realised that it was Good Friday only because the shops in Port Said were closed. He records that he 'was quite forgetful up to today that Lent has been in season'. And although he often gets ashore to Mass, he does not manage it every Sunday, even in port. The last weekend in London he goes to the country, where there will be no Mass.

No wonder he drew for the diary a sketch of a cartoonist's Devil chasing a lad in naval officer's uniform and captioned it: *I'm after you, NTG.* Did the Devil ever catch him? It seems unlikely. Yet the biographical puzzle of the diary remains: how did this man-about-town become the ecclesiastical iron man of later years?

A woman not
for sale

MAUDE O'CONNELL

THE BRITISH TOBACCO COMPANY was once the biggest cigarette manufacturer in Australia. They made all the popular brands, as well as cigars and loose tobacco. Working conditions in their factories were poor and wages were low; but the young women who made up the workforce were too unskilled to do much about this. They needed someone to lead them. They found her in Cecily Maude Mary O'Connell.

A country girl who had lost her mother when she was eleven, Maude O'Connell made her own way in the world. She became a teacher in Melbourne and there got to know some religious sisters who drew her into social work. This led her to puzzle about the harsh working conditions of women and girls: what was it really like in a factory?

To see for herself, she signed on at the big British Tobacco factory. Of course she joined the union and became a shop steward, representing tobacco workers at the Trades Hall Council. At a 1915 Catholic Federation meeting in Melbourne

Town Hall she called for equal education for girls and equal pay for equal work. Archbishop Mannix said it was the first time a lay woman had spoken from the platform at a Catholic meeting.

Thanks to her agitation, conditions got better at British Tobacco. The company decided to neutralise this troublesome shop steward by offering her a job with management. Her reply is preserved in an unpublished biography in Melbourne's La Trobe Library: 'I am not up for sale'.

She was an active member of the Labor Party, winning approval by her willingness to go to the bush and organise. She was an anti-conscriptionist and argued for state aid to church schools, although this was not party policy, speaking in favour of state aid at a public meeting in the Melbourne Town Hall.

When the Catholic Women's Social Guild began in 1916, Maude O'Connell was one of the first to join. The word 'social' in its title did not mean parties or church socials; it meant that the guild aimed to change society by forming lay women into political activists to better the lot of women. Members were expected to join their trade union or professional association and to link up with other women for common causes.

Maude O'Connell became the guild's first fulltime secretary. She and the other leaders organised public meetings about women's wages and working conditions. They spoke at meetings on unemployment and housing and affiliated with the National Council of Women. By 1920 the guild had more than 4500 members.

By this time, Maude O'Connell had moved on to a new phase of her life. She had begun nursing training, perhaps to enable her to accompany the guild president, Dr Mary Glowrey, to India, as a medical missionary. When the great influenza epidemic broke out in 1919, she began nursing the sick in their own homes; and so she stayed in Melbourne.

Her experience of home nursing led her to see that often mothers needed some help in the home. If mothers cracked up, the family would dissolve. What happened when the mother became pregnant again? Who cared for the home then? She saw the need for helpers who would come into homes while the mother was away, either in hospital or even having a holiday. Here was women's welfare work with a difference.

Maude found a sympathetic priest who enabled her to make a beginning in 1930 at Daylesford, seventy miles from Melbourne. Gradually the women who joined her in the work turned their minds to a public religious commitment. They became known as the Grey Sisters because they wore grey uniforms like nurses. At a time when nuns always travelled in pairs, they went about alone, wearing a grey hat, not a veil, and they retained their family name. Home care was always the trademark of the Grey Sisters. In time they added to this mothercraft training, kindergartens, baby health and rest homes for mothers enjoying a spell from the children.

Maude O'Connell did not surrender her interest in politics. In the old days she and Mary Glowrey had found accommodation for girls made homeless through strike action. Now the Great Depression had raised the spectre of jobless women again. So she helped the feminist Muriel Heagney (another convent school girl) organise the Unemployed Girls' Relief Movement, which set up sewing centres where such women could find work. There was thus a radical continuity to Maude O'Connell's life.

A young culture of Catholic practice

MIRIAM AGATHA

THE MOST POPULAR WRITER the *Messenger* magazine ever had was 'Miriam Agatha'. For over 60 years she contributed stories and columns to the magazine and for most of that time was in charge of the children's pages, 'With Our Little Ones'. People went on reading her long after they had ceased to be children. Even bishops were not ashamed to say that they still read Miriam Agatha each month in the *Messenger*.

She wrote about a faith-filled world of good Catholic boys and girls who loved the church and wanted to be saints. They kept the church's seasons of the year, made visits to the Blessed Sacrament at their parish church, saved pennies for the overseas missions, were attentive at school and helpful in the home. It was easy to see what adults savoured in reading about this lost world of innocence.

Children who read Miriam Agatha were led gently into the culture of Catholic practice. They were urged to go to Mass each morning with their brothers and sisters. At home they could encourage the saying of the family rosary. The month of May would bring suggestions for a May altar at home—of course every Catholic school had its May altar then, in some places every schoolroom. Likewise, June would honour the Sacred Heart of Jesus with altars in schools and, at her suggestion, in homes.

Thus Miriam Agatha, year after year, passed on the culture of Catholicism to new boys and girls. Holy water, Stations of the Cross, praying for the Holy Souls, love of the saints and devotion to one's patron saint and guardian angel, Benediction, the Angelus, keeping the nine First Fridays, medals, rosary beads, statues and crucifixes—all of these, and more, were impressed on young imaginations by this skilful writer.

She wrote simply and with sympathy for a child's view of the world. Big words were explained: 'An act of mortification is a going against ourselves—our likes or dislikes'. She remembered too the hazards of childhood. So her readers were told not to make lengthy visits to the Blessed Sacrament, to avoid getting tired. They should make the Stations of the Cross on their own; if they went with friends, they might start giggling.

Her understanding of children prompted her to recommend them to keep 'Acts Books'. These were little notebooks into which they entered the number of prayers they said, their visits to church and acts of mortification. Children's imaginations seized on the 'Acts Books' and longed to fill them. Miriam Agatha never wearied of promoting them. They were especially relevant during Lent. In 1925 she wrote:

'March is a Lenten month. You little children do not fast. But you must abstain [from meat] on Fridays and Wednesdays. You can do many little acts to mortify the appetite—doing without lollies and nice things.'

In the 1960s, although the Lenten regulations had eased, she was saying much the same things, even at times using the same words. And she still encouraged readers to keep an 'Acts Book'. Some things, however, were changing. For decades she had told her children to skip off to the early morning Mass. Now increasingly, she felt she had to warn them of the dangers of road traffic.

Miriam Agatha's real name was Agatha le Breton. The pen-name was chosen on the advice of a priest because she was a school teacher. Born in Maryborough, in Queensland, in 1886, she was taught by the local Sisters of Mercy until the age of 13. Then she became a pupil teacher in Townsville where she wrote her first published stories. As a child, she was always writing something, using whatever bits of paper were at hand. She recalled in 1950 that her favourite writing paper came from grey-white sugar bags cut into squares. She said she still sometimes laughed and even cried when she was writing.

From Townsville, at the age of 15, she sent her first story to the *Messenger*. After it and a few more had appeared, the Reverend Mother at school voiced her disapproval, telling the young writer that her stories were 'merely imitations and not at all original'. Undeterred, Miriam Agatha went on to become the queen of the Catholic magazines. In 1934 she gave up teaching to become a full-time writer. In 1938 she was awarded the papal cross *Pro Ecclesia et Pontifice* in recognition of her services to Catholic popular culture.

Sermons in stone

FR JOHN HAWES

IF THERE IS SUCH A THING as an indigenous Australian church architecture, it can be found in Western Australia. In Geraldton, Carnarvon, Morawa, Mullewa, Northampton, Perenjori and Yalgoo the churches seem to grow out of the earth. Despite many later alterations, their colour, form, texture and placing speak of and to their surroundings. They look quite at home there.

The architect/builder of these churches was an English priest, John Hawes, who spent a quarter of a century in the Geraldton diocese before ending his days as a hermit in the Bahamas. Fr Hawes not only designed churches and other buildings for his diocese; almost single-handed he built some of them himself. When he came to the diocese in 1915, Mass was said in squalid tin sheds. When he left, in 1939, there were a dozen stone churches, including the cathedral, which continue to delight, intrigue and invite the passer-by to stop for a prayer.

The son of a low-church Anglican family, he had been apprenticed by his father to a London firm of architects. Architecture and interest in churches led him away from evangelical religion to high church Anglicanism and ordination. In turn a slum curate, monk, wandering friar and missionary in the Bahamas, he came to Catholicism at the age of 35. Soon he was studying theology in Rome, where he volunteered for the farflung diocese of Geraldton.

He was a popular bush priest, a good horseman, easy with the people and a delight for children. In the bush fashion, he knew he could get a meal at any homestead he visited; his conversation repaid the hospitality. He bred horses and ran them successfully in local races. At least once he won a race himself, when a jockey failed to appear for a ride. In the pub he chatted readily with other horsemen. He was also a dog-lover—when it came time to depart from WA, the hardest wrench was leaving his old dog behind.

Soon after his arrival, the architect priest was brought to Geraldton to build a cathedral. In design the Hawes cathedral speaks strongly of Norman earthiness with traces of Renaissance dash. Its solid pinkish stone ties it closely to its surroundings. The cathedral would take 20 years to build, its stops and starts depending on what money was available. Today St Francis Xavier's Cathedral stands as his monument.

Appointed parish priest at Mullewa, he decided to bring the Dominican Sisters to a corner of the parish to run a school. He would build their convent and chapel himself. Out in the sun all day in the hottest summer on record, his skin became leathery. To soften his hands before saying Mass, he used to anoint them with a mixture of oil and lard. In Mullewa itself he built a parish church and a presbytery.

Like the medieval architects, Hawes liked to work on his creations himself. There was, he felt, something sacramental in letting ideas flow from brain to hand. As he worked, new ideas took over and the design altered, catching the changing rhythms of his poem in stone. Mullewa church, he said later, had been 'a great adventure and a sort of pilgrimage; not something made, but a thing that had grown'.

There were disappointments in his life. Invited by Archbishop Clune of Perth to design a cathedral for the capital, Hawes responded enthusiastically, spending time and energy on the commission and going overseas to secure stained glass, marble and mosaics. At an audience, he presented his plans to Pope Pius XI, who blessed the project. But criticism by local priests, nostalgic for fake Gothic, turned the archbishop against Hawes; and his cathedral was scrapped. A request from Archbishop Mannix for a seminary chapel at Werribee in Victoria met the same fate.

The priest's great supporter was the third bishop of Geraldton, Jim O'Collins, the most dinkum Aussie in the hierarchy. Appointed at the age of 38 as a first fruit of Rome's new policy of making bishops from the ranks of the Australian priesthood, O'Collins had once been a plumber. 'With your architecture and my plumbing, we'll put churches all over the diocese', he said when he met Hawes.

And so, in a sense, they did. When the time came for them to part, it was with genuine sadness on both sides. From his hermitage in the Bahamas, where he lived out the rest of his days, Fr Hawes could reflect on an Australian pastorate that had been rich and fruitful—as his churches still attest.

Something missing

CATHERINE MACKERRAS

THE REFORMS OF THE SECOND VATICAN COUNCIL were not achieved without cost. Many of the pioneers of the great council suffered beforehand because of their ideas and writings. Their books were banned, they were dismissed from teaching posts and denied positions of influence.

After the council, another group of Catholics paid a spiritual tax for the conciliar achievements. These Catholics found the reforms distasteful, inexplicable and destabilising. Many of these were converts to Catholicism who found that some of the things which had attracted them to the church were now changing.

Such was Catherine Brearcliffe Mackerras. Matriarch of the talented Mackerras family, she is a formidable figure in Australian cultural history. With her at its head, the Mackerras dinner table was like a lively university seminar in music, history, literature or philosophy. No wonder the seven Mackerras children—from Charles in music to Malcolm in political studies—have made such notable contributions to Australian life and beyond.

Mrs Mackerras had become a Catholic in 1932. The Vatican II liturgical reforms bewildered her and she resisted them stoutly. She became president of the Latin Mass Society but withdrew after there was some criticism of the Pope. She never liked the English Mass and before she died in 1977 going to Sunday Mass had become more and more of a trial.

The world Mrs Mackerras grew up in was a product of the 19th century. British civilisation seemed the acme of human endeavour. To be British was to be favoured above all other members of the human race. Her father and grandfather, surgeons and great men at the University of Sydney, never questioned the values of the British Empire. Protestantism was the imperial religion, the glue which helped keep it together. To be British was to be Protestant. Nevertheless, they had moved a long way from their familial Presbyterianism, her father in particular. He had ceased to believe; indeed, he had gone on the offensive and in articles and reviews mocked the claims of religion.

As an only child, Catherine was encouraged to read widely. She absorbed the cynicism and agnosticism prominent on her father's bookshelves. But something was missing, she did not know what. The mystery of life pressed in on her, especially when a loved uncle died at Gallipoli. What was it all about?

Her father's books told her that there was no right and wrong, only manners and custom; no truth, only opinions and prejudice; no rhyme or reason to life. It did not satisfy her. She and her father sang in the conservatorium choir and when they were rehearsing Beethoven's *Missa Sollemnis*, she asked him riddling questions on what he thought Beethoven was trying to say in his music. Again she was dissatisfied.

On her own, she kept plugging away. Was truth objective,

a vision of something (or someone) ultimate? Could the human mind arrive at such objective truth? This was a philosophical problem but it had a religious direction.

To this stage, she knew almost nothing about Catholicism. It was the religion of her family's servants, whom she had observed going to daily Mass. It was the religion of the Irish opponents of Empire and so inimical to her family's persuasion. Then she stumbled on a Catholic pamphlet which affirmed the ability of human reason to reach truth, even ultimate truth. Here was a philosophy to underpin religious revelation.

Some time later she had a long, unsatisfactory discussion with her family minister, during which she surprised herself by arguing for the need for church authority, even papal authority. Next, she attended Christmas Midnight Mass at the local parish church. The silent and solemn reverence of the packed congregation made a deep impression. Here, beyond disputes and arguments, was a living expression of true religion.

In a secondhand bookshop she came across a copy of John Henry Newman's classic *Apologia pro vita sua*. The night before, she had read her children the story of Dick Whittington and sung with them the round 'Turn Again, Whittington'. Picking up the secondhand Newman, she opened it and found him quoting the same round.

The coincidence of this hooked her attention and she began to read. How long she stood in the shop reading she could not say. But at the end she knew what she must do. As with so many others in our past, Newman had drawn her into the church.

Adding gold to
the green

FR MAURICE O'REILLY

WHEN FATHER MAURICE O'REILLY CM died in 1933 his admirers from all round Australia sent money to pay for a memorial chapel commemorating his name at Eastwood in Sydney. The O'Reilly memorial chapel was a lofty, handsome building in stone, a fit tribute to one of the best known priests of his day, 'the Dr Mannix of NSW' as he was called. Today the memorial chapel has been converted into a banqueting hall and Maurice O'Reilly is forgotten.

His more enduring memorial is the deep sense of being Australian which is characteristic of Australian Catholics. Historians agree that one of the Catholic contributions to Australian society has been this nationalist sentiment. They credit Maurice O'Reilly as one of the principal contributors to the development.

Coming to this country from Ireland at the end of the 19th century, he sensed Australia was ready to take new directions, away from British imperialism towards a more self-reliant nationhood. When men and women of the Empire tried to establish an annual 'Empire Day' he rebutted them, saying that the celebration should be called 'Australia Day'.

As president of St Stanislaus' College, Bathurst, he developed an annual Australia Day celebration on 24 May which spread to other schools. After High Mass the Australian flag was unfurled and he gave an address on loyalty to Australia. The rest of the day was a holiday, with games, a special dinner and entertainment at night. Elsewhere, school children were calling it Empire Day and saluting the union flag; but in Catholic schools it was Australia Day and the focus was on our own country.

O'Reilly was an occasional poet. A book of his poems was published in 1919 but they lacked staying power. One of them, however, was set to music and became a popular hymn of nationalist Catholics:

> *God bless our lovely morning land!*
> *God keep her with enfolding hand*
> *Close to his side.*

The Australian National Hymn was sung in public for the first time at an Australia Day Mass in the Sydney cathedral in 1912. The year before, Maurice O'Reilly had said in an Australia Day sermon, 'Australia, not England, is our motherland. The flag of Australia comes first with us'. It is easy to understand why historians see him as one of the creators of Australian national sentiment.

Then came World War I. The poet reined in his anti-English sentiment and produced patriotic verses which were widely read. Even Empire loyalists found they could quote Maurice O'Reilly with pleasure. As the war progressed, the question of conscription came to the fore, leading to the two divisive conscription referenda.

O'Reilly was no stranger to public controversy. Neither a subtle nor a penetrating intellect, he was nevertheless a doughty controversialist. On the question of state aid for schools he had clashed with Labour leader W. A. Holman, declaring, 'We are going to sell ourselves to the highest bidder'. Against Protestant and Anglican spokesmen he fired off many letters to the newspapers. So he readily became Archbishop Mannix's lieutenant in NSW during the conscription referenda, defending him from attacks and dissecting claims that Catholics were disloyal. Dissent was not disloyalty, he said.

By now, O'Reilly was rector of the Catholic college at the University of Sydney, St John's. Archbishop Mannix had not wanted him to take the position, believing that his fellow Irishman was too political to be successful there and that the college was too poor to be anything but a heartbreak to him. Yet O'Reilly remained loyal to Mannix and invited him to speak at college functions, although this alienated influential Sydney Catholics. A rich widow, Countess Freehill, was generous in her contributions but the college remained poor. It was the price he paid for his loyalty to the Archbishop of Melbourne.

Maurice O'Reilly stayed at St John's for the rest of his life. The college never amounted to much but it kept him occupied. When a Catholic women's college, Sancta Sophia, was mooted next door, he was unenthusiastic. He considered Sancta Sophia to be no more than a women's hostel somehow affiliated to his own male institution. He put this odd viewpoint into the Latin inscription which the Sacré Coeur nuns asked him to compose for the Sancta Sophia foundation stone. Tactful as ever, the nuns said nothing. But they planted a bush near the offensive foundation stone and soon it could not be read.

The cost of meeting the challenge

Sr DOLORES WHITE

MUCH OF THE STORY OF CATHOLICS IN AUSTRALIA revolves around their schools. Denied state aid, Catholics were determined to keep the schools open. It was a huge challenge; and meeting that challenge was the making of the Catholic community. Its cost, in human resources more than anything else, is easily forgotten. But history is about remembering.

Around the time of World War I it began to be clear that secondary schools would lose their registration unless teachers obtained university qualifications. What to do? Church leaders were unhappy about letting nuns loose in what might be an unfriendly environment. They toyed with the idea of doing a deal with university authorities which would allow a sort of closed-off, nuns-only tertiary institute, but the university people said no. If nuns wanted degrees, they must come to university.

Thus it was that Sister Mary Dolores White OP enrolled in Arts at Sydney University in 1921. From the Maitland district, she had matriculated from the Dominican convent there and, two years later, entered the novitiate. She taught at Maitland and Tamworth before being chosen to be one of the first two Dominicans to enrol at Sydney University. With another nun she would be driven there daily from the order's convent school at Strathfield in Sydney's inner west.

The two Dominicans did brilliantly. At graduation in 1924, they were the only ones to be awarded honours in three subjects. Sister Dolores's final subjects were English, Latin and Philosophy. Overall, she was third in her graduation class. Her honours thesis was on the influence of intellectual equality of the sexes on modern literature. This was an unexpected topic, perhaps. Her approach was unexpected too.

She told, for instance, a story from her schooldays about observing the stars through the school telescope. The northerly pointer of the Southern Cross was a favourite mark of observation: what looked like one star was two stars, thousands of miles apart. Could you put that into a poem?, one girl asked. It's difficult to make a poem out of uncommon facts of science, responded the teacher. Then Dolores heard the girl next to her whisper that the separated stars which looked as one were like a husband and wife who seem to the world to be one but are really quite apart. It was a moment of revelation.

After gaining her Dip Ed, Sister Dolores was sent to the Dominican school at Moss Vale, in the southern highlands of NSW. What spare time this boarding school allowed she gave to working on an MA thesis on poetry. She was interested in new educational methods and gained permission to buy intelligence testing equipment.

She was also in demand at conferences run by the new Catholic Education Association, part of the church's thrust towards higher teaching standards. She told them they should have societies and committees in their schools, so that girls could learn to make speeches, chair meetings and run civic organisations. They should get up to date and not be frightened of the new freedoms for women. Boys schools should wake up too and tell their boys not to begrudge the new liberties women enjoyed. She always gave them something to think about.

But, although no one noticed it, Sister Dolores White was not well. Suddenly and unexpectedly she exhibited signs of mental instability. She was moved from Moss Vale to Mount St Margaret's, a psychiatric hospital in the city. Then, to everyone's surprise, she was dead. She was 37 years old.

The waters of history closed over her head and she was lost to sight. But history has a way of bringing back to life those whom it swallows. Now a history of Santa Sabina College, Strathfield, by Susan Emilsen has restored Dolores White to the fame which is rightly hers. In the book there is a photograph of the two Dominican nuns who went up to Sydney University together in 1921, herself and Sister Anselm O'Brien.

Academically, Sister Anselm was even more brilliant than Dolores, first in her year of graduation, loaded with prizes and honours. She became a notable teacher at Strathfield, a friend of university professors, poets and publishers, whom she invited to the school. Her achievements are honoured with an entry in the *Australian Dictionary of Biography*. But somehow, when you encounter the photograph of these two pioneer university Dominicans, your eye keeps coming back to the troubled face of Dolores White. Part of the cost of the Catholic education system seems hidden there.

Literature for Everyman

P. I. O'LEARY

THERE WAS ONCE A WEEKLY PAPER called *The Advocate* which, from 1868 to 1990, served Australian Catholics well. Published in Melbourne, it never achieved the sales of its Sydney counterpart, *The Catholic Weekly*, which came on the scene in 1942. *The Advocate*, however, was more serious, known for its thoughtful articles and informed commentaries, the opinion-maker of Australian Catholicism. It had a good literary tone.

This was a legacy of a renowned editor, Patrick Ignatius O'Leary, who, by the time he died in 1944 at the age of 56, had won for the *Advocate* the respect of Australia's literary community. Under a variety of names he wrote for every department of the paper, from news to features and book reviews. It was, however, his full-page articles on literature which made his name. Readers responded to his credo that literature was for everyman, not for the elite.

Before the era of mass universities, people got an education by reading books. O'Leary was one of those.

Son of a South Australian teacher, he was lamed as a boy, which enforced long periods of sitting still. So he read. Joseph Conrad and Robert Louis Stevenson adventure stories were early loves, but he also discovered for himself the great poets and Shakespeare. By the time his lameness passed he had caught, as well as the beginnings of an education, the romance of travel from his reading.

Aged 14, he stowed away on a windjammer bound for South America but was discovered and put ashore. Next, he carried a swag on the wallaby track from Adelaide to Broken Hill. He picked up what jobs he could, sent poems and paragraphs to the *Bulletin*, became a shearers' union organiser and joined the staff of the *Barrier Miner*.

O'Leary married in Broken Hill and the young couple then moved to Adelaide, where he got a job on the *Advertiser*. O'Leary was passionate about politics, so when he was heard during the World War I conscription controversy addressing a NO rally outside the *Advertiser* (which supported YES), he got the sack. Lean times. He found work as a time clerk at the BHP Whyalla plant but was soon off to Melbourne in search of a newspaper job. For a time he sold silver polish at a stall in the markets.

Then, in 1920, the *Advocate* put him on its staff, where he remained for the rest of his life. This 'one-man magazine', as his colleague Father James Murtagh called him, had found a home for his wide-ranging talents. His literary essays ran from Donne, Yeats, Joyce or Hopkins to Chris Brennan and 'John O'Brien'. Like many journalists, he wrote against the clock; but his work was never shoddy.

Typical of his winning sympathy was the obituary he wrote on the death of the manager of Melbourne University Press, Frank Wilmot, who wrote poetry under the name of 'Furnley Maurice'. A single sentence, in which each word carries weight, gives the essence of the dead man's personality—so that, reading it, you feel you now know him. Then the obituarist passes to the poetry, which he does not mock by treating it as if it were as good as Shakespeare's.

This obituary appears in a collection of P. I. O'Leary's work, *Bard in Bondage*, put together by his friends ten years after his death. The friends included notable literary figures such as Nettie Palmer and J. K. Moir. Their interest is a sign that, although he wrote for a Catholic paper, O'Leary was neither narrow nor sectarian.

The book's preface is a testimony to his enthusiasm for questions of justice. The most public expression of this was his secretaryship of the Irish Self Determination League— the Irish patriot, Michael Davitt, on a visit to Australia, had been his godfather and all his life he remained a passionate Celt. One of his earliest pieces in the collection is a threnody for the heroes of Easter Week, 1916.

The preface places O'Leary in the tradition of Henry Lawson, whose values, literary and political, he consciously shared: 'the principles of mateship; of solidarity with one's fellows, which is the essence of real fraternity or brotherly love; of charity in relieving a brother who was in need; of thorough honesty in one's dealings with others, whether fellow workers or employers; the belief in the universal brotherhood of man'. This was another legacy Patrick Ignatius O'Leary left to the *Advocate* and its readers.

An uncrowned king

PADDY O'NEILL

A PASSION FOR JUSTICE is one of the contributions Catholics have made to Australia. Its source may be in the convict experience or memories of Ireland or in the social justice encyclicals of the popes—wherever it came from, it is certainly there, and anyone writing about Australian history cannot ignore it.

A good exemplar of this Catholic justice lode in our history is Eugene Patrick O'Neill of Broken Hill. As he lay dying, in 1953, Paddy O'Neill learned that the Pope had conferred on him the cross *Pro Ecclesia et Pontifice* for promoting social justice and industrial peace. Earlier, Cardinal Gilroy, passing through Broken Hill, had called on him to pay his respects to the lay leader. A member of the St Vincent de Paul Society and the Holy Name Society, he was the marshal of Broken Hill's annual Corpus Christi procession.

Paddy O'Neill's Catholic credentials should be stressed from the outset because they underpin everything he did. The son of a dam sinker, he grew up along the banks of the Darling river, spending as much time fishing as he did in school. A local priest took a belt to the boy, to try to persuade him to stay in school. The boy jumped out the window and ran away and that was the end of his schooling.

By then, his father had moved into the carting business. Paddy joined his brothers there, learning to control bullock teams. As a youth he had suffered from a weak chest, but hard work and the outdoor life fixed that. Later he was to become anchorman of a prizewinning tug-of-war team. That was in Broken Hill, where the family finally settled on his 18th birthday.

He soon found his way to the mines. It was chancey work because lodes would run out or the price of metal might drop and men would be sacked. Sometimes your job would be taken by newcomers who offered cash to get a start. A breakdown of equipment meant a stand-down, when you had to wait around because if you weren't there when the starting whistle went, you could lose your job. Paddy O'Neill got to know the system well. He was once out of work for nine months, walking from mine to mine with hundreds of others in hope of a pick-up job.

If you got work, it could be hazardous. Mining companies seemed to show little interest in the health of the men, and accidents in the mines rarely brought compensation. Miners' diseases, like pneumoconiosis and tuberculosis, were regarded as normal risks of the job. Paddy later recalled one family in which five brothers and two brothers-in-law died of miners' complaints.

He thought the way to change these appalling conditions was through effective trade unions. As a young man he was trusted by workmates to put their case to management. This experience of on-the-job negotiation led him to office in one of the mining unions. One of the things he learned there was that there were too many voices speaking for the workers.

They were in danger of cancelling each other out.

In 1899 he had married Mary Anne Gearen. They had four daughters and a son. Being a miner was a precarious way of supporting a family, so in 1913, when a job came up at the city council, he took it. It was a humble position, night soil carter in the sanitary department, a job he kept until three years before his death. He quickly organised council employees into a union, of which he remained secretary all his working life. A humble job and a quite obscure union—yet this man became known as the uncrowned king of Broken Hill.

In 1920 a twenty months' strike ended with victory for the men's claims of shorter hours underground and compensation for miners' diseases. But the strike had revealed sharp disagreements on the union side. Paddy O'Neill set himself to be a healer. It took long negotiations but in 1924 the Barrier Industrial Council (BIC) came into being, with Paddy its president.

For the next 25 years, as BIC president, he was to represent Broken Hill workers in all their negotiations with mining companies. He thought the BIC's strength was that it 'minded its own business', so he kept it away from political ideologies. He saw strikes as a last resort because they hurt people. Instead, he became a matchless negotiator, always feeling for common ground and leaving something for tomorrow. Thus Paddy O'Neill brought justice to Broken Hill.

A woman written
in history

JUDITH BOUWMAN

SHE WAS DUTCH, in her thirties, and she changed the lives of
many Australian women. In Holland she had been a postal
worker. She had gone to some lectures by a scholarly Jesuit,
Jacques van Ginneken, which led her to become a Catholic.

Van Ginneken was a remarkable man, ahead of his time,
you might say. His specialty was linguistics, which he taught
at Nijmegen University. He was also a considerable theologian who had reflected on the lessons to be learnt from
history and anthropology. From anthropology he learnt about
the role of women in matrilineal societies, which contradicted
the womanly stereotypes of recent European centuries.

Despite St Paul and some of the church fathers, he
argued that there were no absolutes in such matters, which
were conditioned by the prevailing culture. In the history of
the church he noted the presence of such powerful women as
Teresa of Avila, Joan of Arc, medieval abbesses and the 12th
century beguines. When he came to the archetypal figure of

Mary, he spoke of her as a strong, capable, independent woman in the home, market place and world of her time. He did not dwell on her as a passive recipient of God's favours or as a submissive spectator of Christ's passion. In the past, he thought, the church had ignored activist elements in Mary's life through fear of women's sexuality.

Van Ginneken dreamed of a women's movement which would speak especially to the women of their own time in a way they recognised. He wanted women to take charge of the culture of Catholicism to express their faith in the symbols of today. In a clericalist church this was very liberating. Women who were energised by van Ginneken's vision formed a new movement in Dutch Catholicism, known as the Grail. Among them was his new convert, Judith Bouwman.

Van Ginneken realised that for the Grail to flourish, it would have to be independent. He advised Grail women to run their own study courses, conferences, retreats and prayer services. Significantly, he advised them not to have chaplains.

In 1936 Judith Bouwman and four other young Dutch women brought the Grail to Australia. Their novelty struck those who met them. They were not nuns, yet they had devoted their whole lives to religion. In the somewhat tense, sin-obsessed, duty-oriented church of the time, their characteristic was joy. These Dutch women seemed happy in their Catholicism. Judith told listeners, 'only a radiant, heroic Catholicism can win the world'.

Later one of her recruits remembered how she would insist that if young Australian Catholic women used their gifts to the full, they would change the world in no time. Another recruit remembered her emphasis on women and culture: men had pushed back the frontiers in the pioneering days; now women must take charge of Australian national culture. In a male-dominated church these were challenging words. As well,

Judith asserted that 'woman is not to be regarded as an appendage of men's movements, societies or other institutions'.

The Grail aimed to produce a new kind of woman for the Australian church. They encouraged such women to think of their futures as being not necessarily defined by marriage. To release their potential, Grail speakers introduced them to great women of the past, including Caroline Chisholm and Mary MacKillop. At the same time they broadened cultural horizons with drama, pageants, choirs, sing-songs, folk dances and even film-making. Thus they tried to get young Australians to see that the faith was something they should own and express for themselves, both personally and communally.

Moving around the Australian church, Judith came to see the need for something more solid than short courses or weekly group meetings. Would it be possible, she wondered, to offer young women the experience of six months integrated living in a residence together? Such an experience would be a course in leadership training; it would give them a taste of community living; and it would help each of them decide what she would do with her life and how she could make religion come alive in her own world. So the decision was taken to open such a residence in Melbourne.

On her way there, in March 1940, Judith Bouwman died in a car crash. After less than four years here, however, she had already written her name into Australian Catholic history.

The good fight, and other fights

NUGENT BULL

LIKE MANY YOUNG PEOPLE IN THE 1930s, Nugent Bull was expecting something big to happen. The promises made after World War I had not been kept. As the world moved through the Depression years, it seemed that society was shaking to pieces. More and more people turned to radical theories, right and left.

Nugent Bull had picked up this wavelength as a boarder at St Joseph's College, the Marist Brothers' school at Hunters Hill in Sydney. There he came under the influence of the lively headmaster, Brother Gerard, who introduced him to Catholic writers like Belloc and Chesterton.

When he left St Joseph's, Nugent joined his parish debating society, and later a new group of young Catholics, the Campion Society. Named for the Elizabethan Jesuit, the Campions analysed the forces that made up the modern world. They were a Catholic response to the intellectual challenges of secularism. At weekends Nugent and his friends would go to the Domain to cross swords with anti-Catholic speakers.

The outbreak of the Spanish Civil War, in July 1936, brought their activities into focus. For them the issue in the war was not fascism versus democracy—after all, in a few years many of them would die for democracy. The issue in Spain, as they saw it, was the Catholic Church against its worst enemies.

The Catholic press was full of atrocities against Spanish nuns and priests. Catholic broadcasters told the same story. Pamphlets with titles like *For God and Spain* and *Red Spain* sold well at church doors. Archbishop Mannix said that Spain was 'a stand-up fight between God and Satan, between Communism and Christianity'.

Within months Australian Catholics had raised more than £7000 to rebuild Spain's burnt-out churches.This was a generous gesture of brotherly solidarity with their fellow-Catholics on the other side of the world. Another expression of such solidarity was that across Australia young Catholics were eager to engage in public debate about Spain. The most famous of these debates was at Melbourne University early in 1937. It ended with the triumphant Catholic war cry *Viva el Christo Rey*—'Long live Christ the King'. In Adelaide, hundreds of Catholic confrontationists stood outside the Town Hall singing *Faith of Our Fathers*.

Stirring times. And Nugent Bull was caught up in it all. But by 1937, then aged 29, he was at a loose end. For a few years after school he had run the family funeral business. Then a change of direction led him into accountancy. In July 1937 he gave up his job and sailed overseas to fight in Spain. 'Pray for me', he wrote to Brother Gerard, as he prepared to take on the cause of Christianity against atheism and communism.

He joined the Spanish Foreign Legion, a tough outfit much feared by its opponents. Daily the legionnaires sang their unit's hymn, 'We are the Bridegrooms of Death'. Nugent was assigned to the Joan of Arc brigade, whose battlecry was 'Long Live Death'. Joan of Arc, he wrote to Brother Gerard, didn't like communism. The only Australian on Franco's side (there were 65 on the other side), Nugent felt elated among the bridegrooms of death, especially as victory was in sight. 'Iberia will be strong in the Church', he wrote.

Then he came down with fever and saw little more of the war. He recovered in time to march in the victory parade through Madrid in May 1939, before going to London. When World War II broke out, he joined the RAF's Bomber Command as a gunner and went down with his plane in September 1940. He was posted missing, presumed dead.

In Spain, Nugent Bull had seen himself as a soldier of Catholicism; in World War II, he laid down his life for democracy.

Divisions in the dressing room

BILL O'REILLY

WHEN BILL O'REILLY DIED, in October 1992, the obituaries revealed a little-known corner of Australian history.

In the golden age of Test cricket, between the world wars, O'Reilly had been a superstar. A ferocious spin bowler, he wrecked England's chances again and again. In four successive Ashes series between Australia and England he took more than 20 wickets per series—a record that still stands. His will to win and unwearying focus during long bowling sessions earned him the nickname 'Tiger'.

Don Bradman called him 'the greatest bowler that I ever faced or saw'; a compliment which O'Reilly returned by saying that Bradman was the best batsman he had ever encountered. Today at the Sydney Cricket Ground there is a Bradman stand and an O'Reilly stand as testimony to their reputations. Yet these two great Australian cricketers were never friends.

Bradman has usually been circumspect about this in public. In his 1985 autobiography, however, O'Reilly discussed the problem frankly. His words are worth recalling in full:

'On the cricket field Bradman and I had the greatest respect for each other. I certainly did for him, and I know he did for me, but I might as well come straight out with it and let you know that, off the field, we had not much in common. You could say we did not like each other, but it would be closer to the truth to say we chose to have little to do with each other.

'I don't really think this arose from the ego-laden encounters of our younger days. It was more the product of the chemistry arising from our different backgrounds. Don Bradman was a teetotaller, ambitious, conservative and meticulous. I was outspoken and gregarious, an equally ambitious young man of Irish descent.'

O'Reilly's measured prose is partly in code because he touches on one of the historic divisions in Australian society, so sensitive that even today historians treat it warily. Nevertheless, to leave it out of an account of where we have been as a nation would be bad history.

Because it shines with undeniable achievements, cricket is a good area in which to explore these tensions coolly and without rancour.

Cricket is an English game, so early Australian teams were made up of men of English descent. After World War I, however, Irish names began to appear in cricket teams and by the 1930s some of them were pushing their way into the national sides: Jack Fingleton, Stan McCabe, Leo O'Brien, Chuck Fleetwood-Smith, Bill O'Reilly—Irish and Catholic.

But the conscription referenda of World War I had, for many Establishment figures, left a question mark over those two words, Irish and Catholic. Were they 'loyal?' Could the Empire 'trust' them? They were certainly different from the majority of Australians and, for some, this difference was sufficient grounds for disliking the minority group. Prime Minister Billy Hughes, in a cynical political exercise, had injected poisonous doses of sectarianism into the Australian electorate, the effects of which were felt long afterwards.

Even in the Australian cricket team, Protestants changed on one side of the dressing room, Catholics on the other. In part, this was a matter of dissimilar temperaments: notice, in the quotation from his autobiography, how O'Reilly characterised Bradman ('teetotaller, conservative, meticulous') and himself ('outspoken, gregarious'). Yet it was more than temperament. And when Bradman became Australian captain, O'Reilly sensed that things might become hotter for him and his mates.

Then something happened which confirmed this vague sense. In January 1937, at the close of a Test match in Melbourne, the Catholics McCabe, O'Brien, Fleetwood-Smith and O'Reilly were summoned to appear before the committee of the Board of Control, all Establishment men, including a stockbroker and a Collins Street specialist. The chairman began to read from a lengthy typewritten document which alleged insubordination, unfitness, slackness in training, etc. But no names were specifically mentioned. Bill O'Reilly interrupted the reading of this bill of complaint: were he and the other three the object of these allegations? No, said the chairman. Then why were they there? So the kangaroo court broke up.

Someone, however, had leaked information to the afternoon papers, who trumpeted the story. Captain Don Bradman always denied having anything to do with the complaints. But since he did not accompany his players to the board meeting, neither O'Reilly nor McCabe, his vice-captain, found these denials easy to believe. So the Catholic-Protestant division in the dressing room remained for another generation to heal.

A country practice

WILLIAM ERNEST WATERFORD

MOST HISTORY IS LOST, especially the history of the laity. Even in this century of the laity, bishops continue to dominate the history books. This is because historians work from episcopal archives, which ensure that bishops get more prominence in the books than they ever did in life. And yet the stories of individual lay men and women are waiting to be told, if only someone would go looking for them.

William Ernest Waterford is a good example. He was a country solicitor in western NSW in the first half of this century. At university he had been a keen debater and as a solicitor he shared fully in the life of the towns where he worked. He was on the local council, serving often as mayor. He helped run the town hospital and ambulance service, as well as sporting amenities such as the bowls club. Horse racing was a special delight to him and he served on several racing bodies.

He got the energy for this public service from his religion. When he died in 1960 his children found in one of his prayerbooks a quotation from the American philosopher Orestes Brownson which he had written there: 'Failure in the performance of one's domestic, social or public duties excludes from heaven as surely as does unbelief or private vice'. Thus W. E. Waterford's public life was sourced in his religion.

He was an observant Catholic. On the death of his first wife (who left him with seven small children) he began to attend Mass daily. Travelling by train overnight to Sydney, he would go to Mass at St Mary's Cathedral before he ate breakfast. He became a member of the Third Order of St Francis, a prayerful lay association. Over many years he developed a strong and enduring prayer life, which he needed as much as food and drink.

There was, however, another side to his Catholicism. As a young man he began to read Hilaire Belloc and G. K. Chesterton, whose writings became a lifelong passion. He had most of their books in his library and he subscribed to Chesteron's magazine, *G. K 's Weekly*. Belloc and Chesterton gave that generation of Catholics courage. A century before, Daniel O'Connell had won Catholic Emancipation by teaching the Irish not to crouch before their oppressors. His biting wit and heroic oratory convinced them that they were as good as anyone. In another age and in other circumstances, Belloc and Chesterton did the same for English-reading Catholics. They gave them confidence in their own case.

So it was no surprise that Waterford, their diligent student, became an early member of the Knights of the Southern Cross. In the crackling sectarianism of the 1920s, such a defensive organisation was a necessity. Not that he was a sectarian—one of his partners in the law practice was a Freemason; and when the Santamaria Movement came on the scene he refused to join it.

His favourite church group was the St Vincent de Paul Society. He liked to say, 'All you can take with you in your cold dead hand is what you have given away'. The SVP enabled him to do that, without fanfare. People, however, couldn't help noticing his generosity. During the Depression, when the police ran out of town men who were on the wallaby track, the men always stopped at Waterford's. There, they knew, you were sure of a feed and a doss-down. Similarly, at his funeral, many Aborigines lined the street and wept at the loss of a friend. Once, for example, he had travelled 100 miles, unasked, to win an acquittal for an Aboriginal charged with boiling his billy during a fire ban. He was, a local paper said, 'a friend to the poor'.

To his children, he tried to communicate his Catholic vision of life. They never forgot the row they got into when he caught them deriding the sanitary man; to William Waterford he was as good as the doctor or dentist. Similarly, he liked to open their eyes to the good (rather than the merely ordinary) qualities in others, such as the battler who distinguished himself by building the best fences in the district. Most of all, his children remembered the depth and sincerity of his religion. 'His faith', they said, 'illuminated his life and gave meaning to every aspect of it.'

Catholics of his generation respected their priests but were not subservient to them. If he disagreed with a sermon, Mr Waterford would collar the priest and argue with him. Often the argument would span several days. He never minded discussing theology with acquaintances. Yet for all the firmness of his personal conviction, as the Anglican rector said in an obituary, no one was more sympathetic or understanding of the other point of view.

The faith that moves Malta

JOSEPH CASSAR

MALTESE PEOPLE ARE A SMALL BUT VITAL element in the story of Australian Catholics. There have been Maltese here since convict days, although it was a century before they made any impact on Australian society as a group. In 1883, 70 men accompanied by a priest went to north Queensland to work on sugar plantations. Conditions there broke their hearts and it was another 20 years before organised migration got under way again.

In the early years of the present century Sir Gerald Strickland, a future prime minister of Malta, was governor of three Australian states and he encouraged migrants from Malta. They were not always welcome. In 1916, for instance, at the time of the first conscription referendum, news of a boat load of Maltese labourers ignited the political atmosphere. Opponents of conscription said cheap labour off such immigrant boats would take the jobs of men who had been conscripted. Such fears closed the door to

Maltese migrants for the next three years.

Then the United States brought in a quota law that restricted entry to its shores. To ease overcrowding in Malta, British authorities pressured Australia to open its doors; and so by the end of the 1920s there were about 3000 Maltese living in Australia. They were market gardeners and poultry farmers, miners, railway men and wharf labourers. In the bigger centres they established social clubs. When they married they usually chose Maltese brides, often bringing them out from home.

Another thing about them: they were intensely religious. The sugar farmers of 1883 had brought their own priest to Queensland, setting the pattern for later arrivals. Fifty years later each sizeable Maltese community had at least one priest from home. Historian Barry York has commented, 'the staunchly Catholic Maltese prefer "homegrown" spiritual comfort. It is very important to the Maltese to have access to Maltese priests in Australia and to be able to confess in Maltese'.

Joseph Cassar was 20 years old when he came to Australia in 1924, one of 682 Maltese migrants that year. He found work at the steelworks in Lithgow, a mountain town west of Sydney, making railway lines and fishplates for the Sydney Harbour Bridge. He was good at his work but everyone knew that the Lithgow steel mills would be moved one day to Port Kembla on the south coast because it had a harbour and was close to coal mines. Joe was asked to move too.

By then he was married—to Mary Vella in the parish church. The Cassars loaded their things on to a cart and walked to the coast, shooting rabbits for food and boiling the billy on the way. In a modest way they prospered; by 1937 they were able to buy their own home. There was plenty of land then, so they bought an extra paddock to grow vegetables. After a while

Joe left the steelworks and sold fruit and vegetables from the back of a truck. Next they got a shop in a new subdivision, Warrawong, where other Maltese families also settled.

Wanting Sunday Mass close to their homes, they persuaded the land developer to let them use the local dance hall. Then they bought the hall and turned it into a church. The 200 members of the Sons of Malta each contributed a shilling a week to the church. Door-to-door collections and Saturday night dances helped too. One Saturday Joe was able to drive to Sydney and pay £27 for a big crucifix for their church. It was a precious moment.

But something more was needed. Joe talked it over with the parish priest and as a result two Maltese Carmelite priests came from Sydney and gave a week-long mission in Maltese. The response was heartening: long queues outside the confessionals and crowds at the altar rails. When Warrawong was made a separate parish, in 1956, it was given into the charge of Maltese Franciscans. For his first three months the new parish priest lived with the Cassars.

Soon there was a Third Order of St Francis, of which Joe was Prefect for 25 years. He also became a catechist at the state school. As an old man he said one of his great joys was to see those he had taught as a catechist still coming to Sunday Mass. 'God blessed me with great faith', he said. 'I'm happy to have been in the heart of community activity in the Warrawong parish.' It was the sort of thing many Maltese pioneers of the Australian Catholic story could have said.

Lay initiatives in Brisbane

JOHN P. KELLY

HOSPITALS ARE OFTEN A FORGOTTEN CHAPTER in Australian Catholic history. A famous doctor or a dedicated nun may find a place in the books, as they deserve, but the institutions they served are left out. This gap in our history is strange since, after the school system, hospitals have been a major Catholic contribution to Australian society.

Looked at in one way, they are big enterprises. Feminist historians have not failed to note that the sisters who founded the hospitals were rare examples of women who were enabled to head large concerns at a time when men ran everything else.

You need more than prayers to run a hospital. Among the talents of the hospital sisters was an ability to persuade prominent lay people to advise them on finance, town planning, legislation and other complex questions outside the usual convent experience. Hospital boards gathered a range of talents to underpin and safeguard the vocation of caring for the sick.

JOHN P. KELLY

John P. Kelly, chairman of the board of the Mater Hospital in Brisbane for more than 40 years, is a good example. He took up the chairman's position at a difficult time in the Mater's history and saw it through to its modern eminence as a great Australian hospital.

When he began as chairman, the State of Queensland had just decided that public hospitals would in future be the concern solely of the state. Other medical centres could register as private hospitals, which in the state's view would be little more than nursing homes. This conflicted with the vocation of the Sisters of Mercy, who believed the Mater should be a public hospital. Under Kelly's leadership they kept their feet in a slippery legislative no-man's-land, surviving and then expanding until a more benign day. Their chairman's skill in negotiation was essential to this triumph of survival.

John Patrick Kelly was a city solicitor who knew little about hospitals when he was asked to serve the Mater. He was, however, already well known to Brisbane Catholics because he was a prominent member of the Christian Brothers Old Boys Association. The Old Boys were enthusiastic debaters. Dozens of members would meet to stretch their brains each week, when everyone was encouraged to have a go from the public platform, rebutting hecklers and answering objections. On some nights they enjoyed formal lectures by specialists or one of their members would open a topic for further discussion. In this atmosphere Kelly thrived.

He came to see that the debaters were being handicapped by lack of books. So, under his leadership, the Aquinas Library came into being. Its initial stock was 63 books stored in a second-hand linen cupboard. But by the time they opened to the public, in March 1933, it had 500 books, which in time grew to a mighty library of 20,000 books.

The Aquinas Library was an answer to the need for a

Catholic follow-up after schooldays. As John P. Kelly said at its foundation, the library aimed to be an institute of higher education in the faith, a 'continuation school' of religious instruction. Its central city rooms became a meeting place for Catholics interested in books and ideas. Thus it is no surprise to find that Brisbane encouraged at this time popular Catholic writers of the calibre of Martin Haley, Paul Grano, James Devaney and Alice Guerin Crist.

Besides the Aquinas Library, the Christian Brothers Old Boys Association (John P. Kelly, President) started a monthly magazine, *The Risen Sun*. Kelly was the editor, writing editorials, book reviews and main articles. The impact of the world-wide Catholic literary revival of the 1930s was clearly seen in its pages and it remains a valuable archive of the Catholic history of its time.

Through this journalism and the library Kelly was picking up new ideas about the role of the laity in the church. These led him to the formation of a dozen Campion Society groups totalling 150 members. Historians credit the Campion Society with being the seedbed of Catholic Action in Australia, which produced a new breed of lay leaders.

At the heart of all this activity was the developing Catholic intelligence of John P. Kelly himself. His success as chairman of the Mater Board won him many deserved tributes. It was also an index of the achievement of the Brisbane Catholicism of his time, of which he was a significant product.

An evangelist for enthusiasm

Br JOHN McELLIGOTT

NOT EVERY GOOD TEACHER is a master of method. Some of the best teachers have been enthusiasts whose passion for their subject spilled across the formal lines of instruction and pushed timetables out of shape. Their pupils caught something of this fire, which illuminated the rest of their lives.

Brother John Evangelist McElligott was like that. When he died at the age of 58 in 1957, his English classes were remembered fondly by Brisbane book collector, Frank Hills: 'He had a deep love of literature, and he transmitted this love to many of his pupils. We did not regard English as just another subject to be studied but as a fine adventure into the world of the poet, the dramatist and the novelist, and surely this is indicative of his greatness as a teacher.'

McElligott grew up in the north Queensland bush, which he knew intimately. All his life he kept his wonder at the marvels of creation. He knew the names of birds and how trees grew and why rivers ran—all of which he could impart to enraptured schoolboys. He had the essential quality of a great teacher, enthusiasm.

His family was poor, his father being a railway ganger who later went on to the land. It was a big family of ten children, who entertained themselves with reading, recitations, stories and bush walks. School was a three-mile walk away, so the little boy was a slow learner. His grades picked up only when they moved closer to a town. At the age of 13 he became a pupil teacher with the Queensland Education Department. This took him to Townsville, where he met Christian Brothers for the first time.

The McElligotts were self-reliant Catholics. Out in the bush, they seldom saw a priest. Indeed, John was not baptised until the age of four, when a passing priest called in to their home. Even when they moved closer to a town, Sunday Mass meant a four-mile walk. There was no Catholic school near them. Their father, however, made sure they knew the faith, preparing them himself for First Holy Communion and Confirmation. When the bishop came round to examine them in the catechism before Confirmation, the parish priest told him, 'You don't have to worry about this four. Their father has belted it into them'.

Well, however it happened, it stuck. Four of the girls became nuns and when John was nearly 17 he announced that he wanted to join the Christian Brothers. His father was against it: the boy was too young, not serious enough, too genial. His mother was on the boy's side: joy was a gift of the Holy Spirit and when God called, you must say *Yes*. He might not call again. So they wore down the father's opposition and at the age of 17 young McElligott went off to the novitiate.

After only one year there, he was sent out to teach. He was to experience a wide variety of schools, in one eight-year period teaching in six communities in the eastern states of

Australia. It was, however, in Queensland that he made his mark and where he is best remembered. Today the Brother J. E. McElligott Memorial Theatre at St Laurence's College, South Brisbane, commemorates this remarkable teacher.

In his own lifetime his quality was recognised by the cultural community. He was a regular broadcaster on ABC schools programs, which brought his expertise to listeners right across Queensland. Surviving scripts, especially those on poetry, reveal a well-stocked mide which enabled him to uncover the hidden riches of the school syllabus and to relate them to English or Australian poetry as a whole. He was a valued member of professional bodies such as the English Association, of which he was president.

Despite such prominence, being a Christian Brother came first with him. He ran the school tuck shop, which gave him a listening post for news of all levels of school life. At times moody and argumentative, he nevertheless participated fully in community doings. He was a champion of young brothers and resisted attempts to regiment them. He was generous in his aid to other teachers who called on his experience, especially at exam times.

At his funeral the priest's words applied signally to him: 'The Christian Brothers are a body of men who live without luxury, labour without emolument, and die without notice, that they might stamp God's image on the soul of youth. That surely is a splendid vocation'.

A rare doctor of divinity

FRANK SHEED

IN BETWEEN THE TWO WORLD WARS, English-speaking Catholics began to notice that there were Catholic books worth reading. That is why church historians name the inter-war years the time of the Catholic literary revival. Close to the centre of the revival was a Sydney man, Frank Sheed. His Marxist father had sent him to Methodist Sunday school, where he got a thorough knowledge of the Bible and a vast repertoire of hymns. To balance this, his Irish mother put him in touch with the Missionaries of the Sacred Heart.

All his life, Sheed would look back on his Sydney youth as a lost Eden of beaches, cricket and fun in the sun. He enjoyed studying law at Sydney University, and tutoring classics at Sydney Grammar School on the side. But, although he topped his year, he came to see that the law was not for him. Years later he told his son that the moment of disillusion came when he learned that some lawyers were paid more than others.

At a loose end, he found his way to London, where he stumbled upon a new lay body, the Catholic Evidence Guild. The guild taught laymen how to stand up in public and speak about their faith. Frank Sheed was quickly hooked. He became a soapbox orator in London's Hyde Park and then brought the idea of the guild back to Sydney, whence it spread to Melbourne. For decades, wherever he found himself, he spent Sunday afternoons on a speaker's pitch.

Catholic Evidence work pushed Sheed to learn more about the faith. Up in public, a pretty smile or good intentions were not enough—you had to know your stuff. He came to see that the church in the English-speaking world had been strong on willpower but had neglected the intellect. He determined to remedy that neglect.

In 1926 he married Maisie Ward, daughter of a family long prominent in English Catholic life. Borrowing money from his mother-in-law, the new husband started a publishing firm, Sheed & Ward. At the other end of town was their only rival, Burns Oates & Washbourne, 'publishers to the Holy See', who specialised in prayer books and Bibles.

Sheed & Ward wanted to make their mark with ideas. At their elbow was the old warhorse, Hilaire Belloc, muttering 'Europe is the Faith and the Faith is Europe'. So they looked across the Channel, and brought home books by Karl Adam, Rudolf Allers, Jacques Maritain, François Mauriac, Paul Claudel, Léon Bloy, Romano Guardini and Nicholas Berdyaev. Those in the know said the Sheed & Ward translations were sometimes better than the originals.

It was a heady mixture. Almost without noticing it, their readers were caught up in international currents of thought and became participants in world-wide debates. The Sheed & Ward net reached as far as Australia, where they found authors such as Frank Letters, Eris O'Brien, J. G. Murtagh and Paul McGuire.

In 1933 they opened an office in New York. There they soon met Dorothy Day and Peter Maurin, co-founders of the Catholic Worker movement, and published their first books. Sheed & Ward also published *God and the Intelligence*, an early work by a young American priest, Fulton Sheen, who would become a national media star but would never write a better book.

Book publishing is a high-risk industry, always teetering on the precipice of financial ruin. Frank Sheed never took a salary from his own firm. To stay alive, he put himself on the American lecture circuit, speaking about what he knew best, Catholicism. The grinding lecture trail gave him an unrivalled knowledge of US presbyteries and colleges. It also gave the young firm much useful publicity and, occasionally, authors they could publish.

Meanwhile Frank Sheed was writing books himself. All those afternoons spent expounding the faith on Catholic Evidence pitches had earned him a simple, direct prose style that could express profound truths in plain language. He did not hide his light under polysyllables. Readers of his masterpiece, *Theology and Sanity* (1947), marvelled at its ability to combine strict rationality with a sense of the wonder and novelty of Christianity. They were not surprised when the Pope made this lay theologian a doctor of divinity—then a rare honour. Nor was this any surprise to the thousands who had learned to think as Catholics from Frank Sheed and Sheed & Ward books.

Wanting to be right

BRUCE MILLISS

ALTHOUGH BRUCE MILLISS DIED in a Catholic hospital, he refused the last sacraments at the end.

For a Catholic, it was a sad conclusion of life that had begun promisingly. Bruce was an altar server, the son of a church family used to looking after the priests who came to their little town. Leaving school, he found work in a haberdashery shop, where he soon made a name for his window displays.

An offer of a pay rise tempted him to a larger town, Katoomba, in the mountains west of Sydney. There he came under the influence of Father St Clair Bridge, the eccentric, rich, brandy-drinking parish priest. Bruce became a daily Mass-goer. Evenings often found him round at the presbytery, playing chess and talking religion with Father Bridge. He became the organiser of the annual St Patrick's Day celebrations at the Town Hall, featuring a dance, supper and a euchre tournament.

The local paper wrote of him: 'He is one of the most active

workers in connection with St Canice's Church, and has gained a popularity with all classes throughout the whole district of the Blue Mountains unsurpassed by anyone'. At times he showed an interest in becoming a priest but Father Bridge talked him out of it.

The parish priest had other plans for this talented young man. In 1922 he turned the parish paper into a monthly magazine for statewide distribution, making Bruce Milliss its editor. *The Record of the Blue Mountains* had a successful two years until church authorities in Sydney told Father Bridge to close it down and devote more time to the. parish. The editor moved back to the retail trade and soon had his own shop.

History, however, was beginning to catch up with the young man. Public spirit had led him into local politics as a member of the Labor Party. Yet Labor seemed to have no cure for the wreckage of the Depression. Always a reader, Bruce Milliss began to search for answers in books that were not in the presbytery library: the Left Book Club, Marx, Engels, Lenin, Stalin.

Personally, he survived the Depression quite well. He owned a draper's shop and a guesthouse and went to Sydney regularly on business trips. But of what use was personal survival when society was breaking up? One day in 1936, in Sydney on business, he impulsively walked into Communist Party headquarters and asked to join. A businessman in a three-piece suit—not your average CP recruit!

Back in Katoomba, he became the nucleus of a secret communist group within the ALP. The energy and leadership he had once put into the parish was now channelled into his new faith. Where once he had read Catholic books, now he studied the classics of Marxism and tried to elucidate them to a new congregation who gathered furtively in the upper room of a secondhand shop. Among themselves, they called him 'The Commissar'.

They stayed inside the Labor Party, pushing it hard to the Left. Locally they fought conservatives on the town council and sponsored initiatives such as a day nursery, a lending library, a parents and citizens federation and, after the war, an Oslo Lunch canteen at the school. Their local MP was Ben Chifley. Bruce Milliss became his most effective campaign organiser, a man who was thought to have the ear of the future prime minister.

But when eventually Chifley did become prime minister, the communists challenged his authority. A series of strikes culminated in the great coal strike of 1949. Faced with national catastrophe, Chifley put the army in to work the mines and ended the strike. By then, however, Bruce Milliss had broken cover. His unremitting attacks on the Labor PM led to his expulsion from the Labor Party.

He moved to Sydney and went into business, importing Soviet films and Chinese tea. The communist businessman was a good contact for anyone wishing to trade with the socialist countries in those Cold War years when such trade was officially interdicted. Business profits boosted party funds. In 1954 he was swept up by the net of the Petrov affair and had his day before the royal commission.

Increasingly he was drawn into the orbit of China, and when that giant fell out with the Soviet Union, Bruce Milliss followed suit. When other Australian communists began to doubt and develop, he adhered to China's Stalinism, as rocksure as any fundamentalist.

In the end, when his old body began to pack up, his sons took him to a Catholic hospital. The priest came round and asked, Did he want the Sacrament of the Sick? 'No way', he answered angrily. 'You can keep your holy oil.' And so he died. On the wall above his bed was an image of the crucified Christ he had rejected 40 years earlier.

Faith knows no jail

Sgt STAN ARNEIL

It is late at night in October 1945 and a tall, thin young man is writing in his diary:

> *11.45 pm: Today has been tumultuous and too much to place on paper. I am home, united with my family.*
>
> *It is very still and very quiet in the house, and as I sit here my thoughts are all of my friends who will never come back as I have done.*
>
> *Thank you, dear God, for watching over me and bringing me home. Thank you, Holy Mary, Mother of God, for the protection you have given me.*
>
> *It is all over now, this diary is finished.*

The diarist was Sergeant Stan Arneil, who had begun keeping a diary in February 1942, when the allied forces in Singapore surrendered to the Imperial Japanese Army. For the next four years Stan Arneil kept his secret diary, carrying it with him wherever he went as a prisoner of war: in Changi prison camp, building the Burma railway and digging tunnels at Johore Bahru across the Straits of Singapore. The diary is a testament to human heroism and the courage of ordinary soldiers.

In Changi the Catholics built a little chapel. There were Stations of the Cross, statues of the Sacred Heart and the Blessed Virgin, a large picture of Our Lady of Perpetual Succour and, on the altar, a tabernacle, flowers and candles. Mass was celebrated there most nights. A young Redemptorist priest got the Legion of Mary going in the camp. Through the Legion all Catholic POWs were contacted and the majority became regular Mass-goers.

Stan Arneil was in the Legion and he didn't need much urging to go to Mass. His love of the Mass grew and it became a real penance to him when he couldn't receive Holy Communion—Mass hosts were scarce, so you went on a roster to receive Communion. He went to Confession regularly too. On the Burma railway you went whenever you met a priest because he might be the last you ever saw.

Sergeant Arneil got to know and respect the POW padres. There was a little Queenslander, Paddy Walsh, who shared the hell of the Burma railway and yet never spoke ill of his captors. There was young Gerard Bourke, the Redemptorist of the early days, who had to wrestle with their moral problems: Could prisoners, for instance, steal from the wharves where they worked? Yes, of course they could, to stay alive.

And there was the Marist, Lionel Marsden, who preached basic Christianity by insisting that the way to repay the Japanese people for their inhumanity was to bring them to Christ. Marsden had a program for postwar reparations: for every Australian who died on the Burma railway they would bring one Japanese to Christ and so make all those deaths worthwhile. (Father Marsden showed he meant it. Three years after the war he opened a Marist mission in Japan with Stan Arneil's help.)

Having survived the Burma railway, Arneil found himself back in the comparative comfort of Changi . There was still a roster for Communion hosts but on Sunday evenings he could attend Benediction of the Most Blessed Sacrament as the sun set over the prison yard. Volunteers decorated the chapel with flowers and shrubs, A different padre gave the Benediction sermon each Sundav. The sergeant noticed that he looked forward to a good sermon and enjoyed following it without constantly consulting his watch. Perhaps, he noted in his diary, he was growing up.

Then, for the last few months of the war, he was shifted across the Straits of Singapore to dig hold-out tunnels for the Japanese. There was no padre there, so the men organised a nightly recitation of the rosary, beginning on Good Friday 1945. They used rosary beads made by one of their mates.

For the historian, the account in Stan Arneil's secret diary of those priestless POWs keeping their faith alive by saying the rosary together at night is a flashback to the earliest Australian Catholics. They too were prisoners without priests. Somehow they too kept their Catholic faith alive as lay people. It is a part of the Australian Catholic tradition that, as Stan Arneil's diary shows, never died.

Our second saint

DAMIEN PARER

IF AUSTRALIAN CATHOLICS ARE LOOKING for a second saint to put
alongside Mary MacKillop, they might consider Damien Parer,
the World War II cameraman. The first Australian to win an
Academy Award, Parer's memory has been kept green by film
lovers.

He learnt his craft in the early days of the Australian movie
industry, under such pioneers as Charles Chauvel and Ken G.
Hall. When war came, he quickly joined a film unit, taking his
camera to the North African desert, Palestine, Greece and
Syria. In 1942 he went north to the jungles of Papua New
Guinea, where he shot his most famous documentaries.

To him, the heroes of the war were the rank and file of the
infantry, whom he knew intimately. He learned to get in front
of them as they advanced, to catch the light in their eyes; but
he would also film them off-duty when the light faded. He
thought their mateship, like that of the original Anzacs, was
the binding force of the army and that it said something

essential about Australia. Parer was the Henry Lawson of war-time newsreels.

Yet government bureaucrats made life difficult for him until, frustrated, he resigned and went to work for the Americans. He was filming an American advance in the islands, ahead of the troops as usual, when, aged 32, he was hit by machine-gun fire and died.

The extraordinary thing about Damien Parer was that everyone who knew him recognised and spoke about the religious dimensions of his life. It wasn't just that he said his prayers regularly—he certainly did that without embarrass-ment or affectation, wherever he was, in a troopship cabin, a military barracks or by a jungle track. He was a regular, even daily, Mass-goer and communicant. He had a devotion to the Blessed Virgin Mary and a love of the rosary.

Well, other young Australians have had exemplary prayer lives. What was special about Damien Parer was the way he saw his work as an expression of his love of God. He was like the medieval juggler who offered his best juggling as a prayer to the Mother of God. Damien polished his lenses, cared for his equipment and used it to the limits of his ability because he knew that was what God wanted of him. His vocation as a cameraman was as real as a vocation to the priesthood.

Colleagues knew this was genuine, for their world-weary eyes had watched him closely. 'Of all the people I know', said one colleague, 'he probably lived closer to the Sermon on the Mount than anyone.' An example of this was his practice of spending part of his leave in Australia visiting the families of men at the front. In the field he carried ammunition to the men in action and volunteered to go out and rescue wounded soldiers. He treated PNG indigenes as human equals—an attitude which was then rare.

He had faults, of course. One was a low-level anti-Semitism, the sort of virus you picked up unconsciously in Australian society then. In Palestine, Parer got to know individual Jews for the first time and he saw that his anti-Semitism was a prejudice he must eradicate.

In this he was helped by friendship with an Anglican padre, Fred Burt, who encouraged him to visit kibbutzim and introduced him to Jewish families. Parer and his best mate, Maslyn Williams, would take Burt out for a night of song, wine and poetry. They learned tolerance from this genial Anglican; and he learned to enjoy himself with them.

For Parer rejoiced in life. He had a memorable laugh—a hoot someone called it, a donkey laugh Maslyn Williams said—which was often heard at parties. He enjoyed playing cards and when he lost he seemed to think it a huge joke. He liked women's company and they liked him too, although one of his colleagues noticed that he had a quality he called 'untouchability'.

In any case, there was already someone he loved, the beautiful Marie Cotter, whom he married early in 1944. They had a short honeymoon, during which he dragged her off to the movies as often as possible. When he came on leave again she told him she was pregnant. But he was never to see his son because before the year was out Damien Parer was dead. His widow received hundreds of letters, each from somebody who seemed to have lost a personal friend.

God's eyes and ears, hands and feet

Sʀ KATHLEEN DALY

Wʜᴇɴ Kᴀᴛʜʟᴇᴇɴ Dᴀʟʏ ᴡᴀs ᴀ ɴᴏᴠɪᴄᴇ in the Sisters of St John of God at Broome (WA), she and the other novices went for a walk one day down to the jetty, where they saw an Aborigine scarred by leprosy. The sight shocked them and they wondered where they would gain the stamina and goodwill to care for lepers.

Kathleen never forgot that first sight of the dread disease. She would become Sister Mary Alphonsus and spend 36 years of her life among lepers. Her work would be honoured by an MBE and she would become one of the first nurses in WA to be made an honorary fellow of the Australian College of Nursing. It was a life of quiet heroism that deserves to be remembered.

Her path to heroism was a winding one. A member of a Melbourne family of twelve, she somehow heard of a small group of sisters working in the Kimberleys among Aborigines and mixed races. Joining the sisters in 1912, she became a music teacher in their school at Broome. Life was hard in a two-roomed galvanised iron convent: not much food, heat, sandflies, fierce mosquitoes. 'If only we could get a net or two', they joked, 'we could use them in turns to get a good night's sleep.' They put smoking sticks in cans and they burnt manure, but still the mosquitoes persisted.

When World War II came and Broome suffered air attacks, they were ordered south, but the sisters refused to leave those to whom they had devoted their lives. For safety they were sent 80 miles north of Broome to the Beagle Bay mission, where 500 refugees congregated. Soon after their arrival, Sister Alphonsus was involved in one of the odd episodes of the war.

Indonesia was then a Dutch colony. With the threat of Japanese invasion, Dutch civilians were flown to Australia. Just before takeoff, Captain Ivan Smirnoff was given a mysterious box to be collected at the other end. Unknown to the pilot, the box was full of diamonds, which a bank in Java meant to keep out of enemy hands.

Before the diamonds could be delivered, however, Smirnoff's plane was attacked by Japanese fighters on their way to Broome. He crash-landed on a beach and survivors were brought to the mission at Beagle Bay, where they were restored to health. Smirnoff's biographer pays tribute to Sister Alphonsus' care, calling her 'a motherly woman'. (The diamonds, incidentally, were never recovered—giving rise to many local stories.)

By then, Sister Alphonsus was a fully qualified nurse. In 1944 her superiors appointed her to the Derby leprosarium. Opened in 1937, it was regarded as 'the best and most up-to-date in the Commonwealth'.

Formerly, leprosy sufferers had been sent to Darwin—a cruel punishment for Aborigines, to be expelled from tribal lands. Several times the sisters had petitioned to be able to work with lepers but their wishes had always been frustrated by unsympathetic government officials. Now, with leprosy on the increase, the government turned to them.

The historian of leprosy in WA, W. S. Davidson, credits their work at Derby as being an important factor in the control of the disease. They made it possible for sufferers to resume normal lives in the community. In 1951 there were 333 patients at Derby; in 1975, 23. Dr Davidson argues that the sisters' continuity of residence there ensured a continuity of knowledge and experience.

He must have had Sister Alphonsus' 36 years at Derby in mind, for she stayed there almost until the day she died in 1980. There was nothing much for patients to do at the leprosarium, so she brought them music.

Her orchestra began with five donated violins. The first five players encouraged others and more instruments had to be found. In time, they had 40 violins, six banjos, one cello and a cornet. Beethoven, Mozart, Wagner and Handel were in their repertoire, as well as dance music and jazz. The humid weather wrecked their instruments and insects ate the hair of their bows. No matter, Sister Alphonsus' leper orchestra played across the years.

At the end of her life she obeyed her superior's request and wrote a short memoir. A sentence about Broome, 1912, could stand as an epitaph for the whole of her heroic life: 'We lived out our every-dayness convinced that we were there to do God's work—to be His eyes, His ears, His hands, His feet.'

'A priest who was one of us ...'

Fr LIONEL MARSDEN

THE MEN WHO SURVIVED the Burma-Thailand railway in World War II often spoke of Father Lionel Marsden. The young Marist priest had gone with them into the jungle and stayed beside them, giving them courage, the will to survive and, if need be, a prayer at the end. He persuaded their captors to allow him to move along the railway line as it was being built, in order to visit work camps where there was no priest. At the end of the day, after trudging through mud with his Mass kit on his back, he did not sink to exhausted rest. No—that was when his work began.

The POWs knew he did it for them and revered him for it. After the war, one of them wrote: 'Life without the priest was too awful to contemplate, as we never knew whose wasted body would next be thrown on the funeral pyre. We were lucky in that respect—we had our priest, Father Lionel Marsden, quite young, in fact not much older than the youngest of us.

'It was a big responsibility for him, all those men depending on his efforts, and he did not spare himself. He was our mainstay and we regarded him as children would a loving father. Ever at our beck and call, he never complained but listened to our hopes and fears whenever we wanted to talk. Looking back now, we realised that he had nobody to whom he himself could turn. He needed, in his loneliness, all the strength of his great vocation.'

When war ended, Marsden did not speak of his own exploits. In a long interview he gave to the editor of the *Catholic Weekly* in 1945, he spoke of what others had done. Especially he praised the devotion of Dr Kevin Fagan, who kept men alive in such difficult circumstances. He told how Fagan had moved along the line of men as they marched into Thailand, patching them up as they went—for their guards would not let them fall out for medical attention. In rest periods Dr Fagan did not relax; that was when he worked flat out to keep them alive. By the end of that long march the doctor was a legend.

In his interview Marsden remembered the day he had seen Fagan come out of the medical tent looking worried. 'What's up?' he asked. 'I think we have our first case of cholera in there', came the reply. Cholera—it was what everyone feared and, true to expectations, it cut down the POWs mercilessly.

Each morning those not on work parties would go to the cemetery and start digging graves. Then would come a call to the chaplain to hurry back to camp because someone was dying. At one work camp in one day alone they buried eight Australians. Then the Japanese became afraid of catching cholera themselves, so they ordered all bodies to be burnt. Afterwards, Marsden's men would build a chapel to commemorate those they left behind.

In some lives there are special moments when God seems to call us to a difficult task. For Lionel Marsden that moment of election seemed to come while he was saying Mass in the pre-dawn by the light of two small candles. Just then, a battalion of Japanese fighting men marched out of the jungle with flaming torches and singing war chants to their gods. As they passed by his flimsy altar and tiny, ragged congregation, the words of Jesus came into his mind: 'Go, teach all nations, baptising them in the name of the Father and of the Son and of the Holy Spirit'.

From this grew a determination not to waste his wartime experience. He began to say to the men that they (meaning, perhaps, himself?) should try to convert one Japanese to Christ for every Australian who died in captivity. He told them not to hate the Japanese because to do so would make them equals in moral squalor. The men found this a hard saying but they respected him for it. One of them recalled: 'The short sermons he gave we thought about for days afterwards. He could speak, that young man, not as an elevated faraway person, but as a priest who was a soldier and one of us'.

After the war, Lionel Marsden showed that he meant what he said. He became a missionary in Japan and spent the rest of his life trying to bring his former captors to Christ.

Shut out but
still heard

MARY TENISON WOODS

THE NAME TENISON WOODS IS WELL-KNOWN to Australian Catholics. Father Julian Tenison Woods is famous as co-founder of the Sisters of St Joseph. Another Tenison Woods deserves to be better known than she is. This is Mrs Mary Tenison Woods, pioneer feminist and woman lawyer.

In 1916 she became the first woman in South Australia to graduate in law. Nine years later, she established her own legal firm with Dorothy Somerville—thought to be the first female law practice in Australia.

By then she had married a cousin of Father Julian Tenison Woods. The marriage was unsuccessful, the couple separating after a few years. There was one child, a son known as 'Mac', who was slightly disabled.

Her son's disability sharpened her interest in child welfare matters. It became, she said, the love of her life. 'I came to feel that any child could become a delinquent, even, but for the grace of God, my own redhaired son.'

Moving to Sydney, she became an editor of law books, which allowed her time to follow other interests as well as to care for her son. Her book *Juvenile Delinquency* (1937) emphasised the need for rehabilitation rather than punishment of young offenders. It argued that before imposing senrences court should take advice from psychiatrists, psychologists and social workers.

She won increasing recognition for her views on social work and was appointed to a string of advisory bodies. She became a part-time lecturer at Sydney University and, in 1947, was guest speaker at the first Australian conference on social work. People in the field found her a warm, sympathetic champion. Mary Tenison Woods' tireless advisory work, matched by her argumentative strengths and a skilled use of the press, led to the establishing of a Child Welfare Department in New South Wales, separate from the Education Department.

Her friends were Catholic women like herself: Jean Daly, also a lawyer, who ran the successful wartime Navy Club near Circular Quay; Norma Parker, pioneer social worker and lecturer in social studies at Sydney University; Phyllis Burke, an economist with the NSW Housing Commission; and Mary Whitton Flynn, whose reading put her in touch with a wide range of overseas opinion.

In 1944 the Catholic bishops issued a social justice statement, *The Family*. In a recent study, Professor Michael Hogan finds that the statement's section on women, called 'The Woman of the House', argued that a woman's place was in the home and not in the general workforce. Revealingly, the section on men was titled 'The Head of the Family'.

Mary Tenison Woods and her friends sat down and-read the bishops' statement. When they had finished they wrote to their archbishop, Dr Norman Gilroy, to tell him what they thought of it. In particular, the group noted 'the absence of the woman's point of view' in the statement. They thought references to 'the dignity of domestic service' and the need to instil this in girls through 'homemaker' courses were ignorant and and romantic . They criticised the statement's lack of enthusiasm for nurseries and its masculinist discussion of divorce. They were very courteous but it was clear they were not impressed. Archbishop Gilroy did not bother to respond to their criticisms.

The group continued to meet and by 1946 they were ready to form themselves into a section of the St Joan's Social and Political Alliance, an international Catholic women's movement. They wrote to inform the Archbishop, by now a cardinal, asking for his blessing. Cardinal Gilroy withheld his recognition. In vain did the members appeal to a recent call by the Pope for women to play a more active part in public life. The Cardinal let it be known through the parishes that membership of the alliance was contrary to his wishes. *The Catholic Weekly* refused to publish the alliance's publicity releases.

Despite this rebuff, it continued as a ginger group, with a membership of about 100. Mary Tenison Woods described it as 'a body of Catholic citizens acting as citizens … wherever the status and interests of women are concerned'. The government took notice of it. In 1950 it sent Mary Tenison Woods to head the status of women office at the United Nations secretariat in New York.

When she left the United Nations, eight years later, delegates praised her dedication to the cause of women and her team qualities. For Australian Catholics, however, there is another side to her story: clericalist refusal to accept an intelligent Catholic feminist.

A layman's mission

FRANK McGARRY

WHEN FRANK MCGARRY DIED in 1955, people who knew him said he was the greatest missionary Australia had ever seen. For 13 years he had lived with Aborigines around Alice Springs, pioneering the Catholic mission there.

He went to Alice Springs in 1935 to help Father Patrick Moloney MSC get started. At first they were at a bit of a loose end, unsure how to begin. Frank visited the Halfcaste Home and the Blacks' Hospital, a tin shed two miles out of town. He took over the Sunday morning catechism classes in the presbytery—although some white parents objected to their children mixing with Aboriginal Catholics.

He was getting to know the people but it was frustrating work because it did not seem to lead anywhere. After six months of this, the frustration blew its head on the feast of St Thérèse of Lisieux, the Little Flower, to whom both priest and layman had special devotion.

Expecting a sign of favour on her day, they drove out of

town until they contacted some Aborigines. Coming straight to the point, Father Moloney told them he wanted to start a mission for them. Would they accept? Yes; and to prove it, here were ten of their children to be baptised. The priest baptised them straight away, with Frank as godfather. Anthropologist Eugene Stockton has said that Father Moloney's readiness to baptise Aborigines after little instruction, while criticised by his colleagues, 'was vindicated by lasting results over generations'.

Now the real work could begin. Frank gathered the Aboriginal children into the presbytery for daily lessons, feeding them and tending their sores while they were there. Adults began to come too, although the law forbade fullblood Aborigines from entering the town unless they had work. Within a few weeks there were more than 30 Aborigines, adults and children, at the presbytery each day. Frank fed them by begging food round town. From Mick Heenan, the market gardener, he got tomatoes, cucumbers, pumpkins and bruised fruit. The town baker gave him surplus bread and from the butcher he got bones and meat trimmings. All of these he collected himself, walking through Alice Springs with a gunny sack over his shoulder.

There was no 'side' to Frank McGarry. Likewise, he bore the open enmity of townspeople who on principle disliked 'black-mixing'. 'It doesn't matter what people say or think', he wrote home, 'we're working for God.'

Nevertheless, he knew he would have to get the mission on to its own bit of land, away from the presbytery. The chance came with a government offer of land on the outskirts of Alice Springs. Here the Little Flower Mission became actual, with Frank McGarry at its heart. By the time Father Moloney was transferred to eastern Australia early in 1939, the mission was thriving.

The coming of war put pressure on land around Alice Springs, so in 1942 they moved to Artlunga, 68 miles away. Frank went out to this distant post and for many months was the only white person there. Then he was joined by clergy and sisters as the mission settled down to a daily routine.

Lay missionaries have to learn that priests, sisters and brothers are human beings like everyone else, with everyone's human failings. Frank McGarry had learnt that earlier when Father Moloney went on leave and a replacement priest had tried to exclude him from the mission. The exclusion order was rescinded but not before its injustice had reduced the layman to tears.

Now, in 1944, the same thing happened again: he was told he was no longer wanted. To continue his service of the Aborigines he loved, he joined the Department of Native Affairs. On remote posts he battled disease, hunger and outbreaks of violence. The Devil whispered in his ear that it was too hard; he should give up and go home to the seaside at Manly, in Sydney. He shut his ears to the whisperings until his health broke and the decision was taken out of his hands. As usual, he accepted this. His life, after all, was at God's disposal.

Winning the peace

Mother MARY SHELDON

Australian nuns who lived through World War II in Japan helped rebuild Japanese society after the war. They were Religious of the Sacred Heart, an order which had gone to Japan from Australia in 1908.

At the opening of their International School in 1948, Prince Kuni of the Japanese imperial family spoke words of high praise: 'I admire the nuns of the Sacred Heart; they remained at their post during the difficult years of the war, to continue their work for our youth. They lost a great deal in 1945, but, in spite of that, they have kept up their fine school at Sankocho, and now they have the courage to begin this new, valuable work.'

Throughout those war years the Sacré Coeur nuns were led by Armidale-born Mother Mary Sheldon. Following her education at their Rose Bay Convent on Sydney Harbour, she had entered the order at the age of 22. After teaching at Rose Bay, Melbourne and Auckland, she was sent to Tokyo on the sudden death of the local superior. Mother Sheldon was to remain there until her death 37 years later, without visiting her homeland again.

Her work in the Sacré Coeur school at Sankocho, a suburb of Tokyo, and in their other schools was in some ways in advance of its time. Her aim was not to westernise the girls but to make them more Japanese. Visits to national parks and the principal sites of historic events were part of their curriculum . She studied Japanese history and culture in order to infuse her pupils with the best and noblest in their own tradition. The ancient Japanese sport of women's fencing was taught, to encourage alert minds and supple bodies. On the archery range the acquiring of grace was as important as good markmanship. In the tea ceremony house the antique etiquette of taking tea was transmitted to future generations of leaders.

Mother Sheldon recruited Japanese teachers to her staff and she encouraged Japanese women to join the Sacré Coeur order. There were good theological grounds for this policy but it also had unexpected benefits after the outbreak of war. For the war put pressure on the foreign nuns. Some were interned, while others remained in their converts under virtual house arrest. Public positions were taken over by Japanese nuns and teachers, the foreigners keeping discreetly in the background.

Mother Sheldon found difficulties in fulfilling her normal tasks as provincial. Cut off from all but minimal contact with many of her nuns, she committed their care to God. To free Japanese for public roles such as teaching, she turned to doing the housework, cleaning, kitchen work, hauling water and gathering firewood. The strain told on her eyesight and for a time she could neither read nor write. Throughout all this her trust in God never wavered. Once she gave away their milk and sugar to a suppliant mother, saying, 'Don't be troubled; God will give it back to us'. She was not surprised when they had twice as much before the day was out. 'This has often happened to me', she said.

As the war came home to Japan, the Sacré Coeur nuns suffered with everyone else. Food was in short supply. There were no shoes, so they wore peasant straw sandals. And always, the bombing. The Sankocho convent in Tokyo was flattened and the nuns evacuated. There were nuns in Nagasaki when the atom bomb fell there on the morning of 9 August 1945. One of them has left a graphic description of the hum of an unseen solitary plane, the strange silence followed by a fearful explosion and everything turning to the colour of gold, as if the sun had burst.

Eight days later, in the middle of the night they were summoned to the dining room. Two guards and officials came in, then the chief officer spoke: 'Congratulations! The war is over. We have been defeated and you are the victors. Let us all shake hands and celebrate'. The nuns were stunned and anxious to return to bed; but their guards wanted to party on.

Mother Sheldon started to rebuild immediately. She had been through it all before, in the aftermath of the horrendous 1923 earthquake when the Sacré Coeur nuns had lost almost all their Tokyo buildings. Then, she had turned to Japanese friends for support, which they gave generously. Now Australia rallied to her cause. By September there were 29 giant packing cases on the water to Japan, followed later by five splendid Jersey cows.

So the Sacré Coeur nuns were able to play their part in the rebuilding of Japanese society. Mother Sheldon reminded her nuns that at the outbreak of war they had put their trust in God's providence. Not one of them had been injured, even slightly. Their trust in God had not been breached.

A Grail found and never lost

ELIZABETH REID

AN AUSTRALIAN WOMAN HELPED TO BUILD UP THE CHURCH in Hong Kong in the years after World War II. She was Elizabeth Reid, a journalist from Queensland who was recruited to run the local Catholic paper, *The Sunday Examiner*. It was a one-woman paper, on which she was editor, designer, photographer, advertising executive and sales manager. For seven years she was a vital element in Hong Kong Catholicism.

Before leaving Australia, in 1948, she had gone to see a veteran Columban missionary, Father Gerry O'Collins (uncle of today's Jesuit theologian of the same name who teaches in Rome). He told her, 'Your function in Hong Kong is to be a bridge. You will be serving the church only if you prepare local people to take your place—and it shouldn't take too long! You must prepare Chinese girls to play their part in the apostolate of the church, christianising the various levels and structures of society'.

Very soon Elizabeth Reid had started a students' press

group, who had their own paper, *The Hong Kong Student*. It was great fun but there was a serious side to it too, as the students learned to be journalists and at the same time explored the meaning of Catholicism with their mentor. The group became a point of contact with other young Chinese, who would become Catholics of the future.

Elizabeth lived in a Catholic parish in Hong Kong, sharing her tiny house with other young women. Whatever they had they held in common. Meals were times for discussion and each evening they prepared the gospel of the next morning's Mass, which they attended together.

Her years in Hong Kong coincided with the communist victory in China, a time of persecution for Catholics. She was part of the team from the Catholic Centre who conducted a daily watch at the border for those expelled from the new China. Her journalism was filled with their stories of harshness and despoliation, interleaved with confidence in the heroic Christians they had been forced to leave behind.

Those thousands of refugees were a vast challenge to the church in Hong Kong, which found places for them to stay, food and drink, a future. The encounter was never one-way, for coming across the border were tested martyrs to the faith. Their impact would be felt in Hong Kong for many years to come.

For Elizabeth Reid, each day was like living through a cyclone. Once a month she got away for a day of silence and reflection, to realign her spiritual compass. She had been used to doing that ever since she joined the Grail movement back in Australia.

After schooldays at Lourdes Hill convent in Brisbane, she had trained as a nurse at the Royal Brisbane Hospital. One night she saw a film about a new Catholic movement for women, the Grail. Attracted by what she saw, she went down to Sydney to a summer school and what she heard there changed her life. The Grail challenged women to become more than homemakers and docile parishioners. Private piety was not enough, it said; together we can change the world. It was joyful, lively and hopeful religion; and it caught the attention of hundreds of Australian women.

Elizabeth was one of the first to join, in 1939, when she was 24 years old. Soon she was in Melbourne, at the Grail's adult education centre running formation courses for future women's leaders. When a national Catholic girls' movement began, she became a full-time organiser and editor of the movement's magazine, *Torchlight*.

You might have predicted that she would become a journalist, because her father had been editor of the Brisbane *Telegraph*. Bushwalking with him, her mind was filled with stories of life overseas and Reid family history. He told her of his war experiences at Gallipoli and in France, of devastated cities and hungry people. From her father she got a political sense, especially of the injustice of the White Australia policy. So she began to write.

Journalism took her to many places in the Third World. She covered, for example, the historic 1955 Bandung conference of Asian-African nations. On her way to the conference she renewed contact with Maria Malone, the first Australian to join the Grail, who by then was teaching English in Indonesia.

Wherever Elizabeth went as a journalist, there were women like herself, formed by the Grail to be adult in their faith and alert to the needs of their world.

A Minister for survivors

ARTHUR CALWELL

THE SYDNEY JEWISH MUSEUM, as the one in Melbourne, is a sombre memorial to evil in the 20th century. To those brave enough to enter its doors, it presents the horror of the Holocaust through pictures, texts, videos and pathetic small souvenirs of the death camps. There can be no better place in Australia to meditate on the reality of sin.

To a non-Jew, one text in particular brings home the everyday nature of what the museum is about: 'Ordinary people, not monsters or psychopaths, made the Holocaust'. That is to say, while the idea for the extermination of Jews may have germinated in the mind of Adolf Hitler, its execution needed the willing cooperation of tens of thousands of ordinary men and women—people like us.

To what extent individuals are swept along by history, and to what extent they can shape history, are questions posed here. To those meditating on such uncomfortable questions, another text in the museum's display offers some relief. It asserts that individuals can do something towards making the world a better place. It reads: 'After Israel, Australia accepted the second highest number of Holocaust survivors'.

Of course, this raises more questions. Who was a 'Holocaust survivor'? What about the US intake? Who's counting? But beyond such queries, the museum text points to a forgotten episode in Australian history which shows that in the long run individuals can shape the history of their own times.

Before World War II, the Australian government had agreed to accept 15,000 Jewish refugees from Hitler's Europe. Some 7000-8000 of these arrived before the outbreak of war closed the sealanes. During the war several thousand more arrived, curiously classified as 'enemy aliens'. Many of these were to become creative contributors to post-war civic, academic and cultural life. As the war ended, leaders of Australian Jewry turned their attention to survivors of the European experience. Would Australia offer them a home?

They found an Australian politician willing to listen to their entreaties. He was Arthur Augustus Calwell, Labor member of federal parliament for Melbourne. An observant traditionalist Catholic, he was close to Archbishop Mannix, who was himself sympathetic to Jewish causes and had Jewish friends.

In July 1945, Calwell became Minister for Immigration, the first in our history. The new minister was keen to expand population through immigration. By the time he left office, in December 1949, Australia was receiving 150,000 immigrants per year. Preference went to British migrants; but when they proved hard to get, the minister went elsewhere in Europe for his new settlers, or 'New Australians' as he encouraged people to call them. Historians see Arthur Calwell as one of the architects of modern Australia.

When Jewish leaders came to him with their rescue plans for Holocaust survivors, he was immediately sympathetic.

Warily he set limits to their plans. Only immediate relatives of Australian Jews could come. The community itself must organise the transport and care of survivors. Paperwork would be done in Jewish welfare offices. As in the past, there would be a quota: this time, not more than 25 per cent of Jews on any migrant ship.

The Jewish leaders agreed with these restrictions, noting that the ultimate test of an immigration policy was the needs of Australia. So Calwell persuaded Prime Minister Ben Chifley and his colleagues to back the policy. By 1946 permits had been issued to 2000 Jewish refugees on a humanitarian basis. In April of that year the first ship arrived.

Calwell had been right to be wary. Populist politicians protested at the arrival of the refugees. Newspapers ran racist cartoons and stories. The press carried a photo of an 84-year-old woman being brought ashore on a stretcher to rejoin her family. 'The sort of migrant Mr Calwell is bringing to this country', said the caption. Preference should go to British ex-servicemen not 'aliens', said RSL leaders. Later, Jewish atrocities against British servicemen in Palestine would seem relevant. Despite the Holocaust, anti-Semitism was never far away.

Modern Jewish historians tend to emphasise the restrictive side of Calwell's policy, such as the 25 per cent quota. Contemporary community leaders, on the other hand, knew that the minister had read the political weather chart accurately and gave him credit for it. In gratitude, they put his name on buildings in Israel. They knew he was one individual who had done something about the Holocaust.

Raising a woman's voice

MARY RYAN

MARY MARGARET RYAN CAME FROM A FAMILY of eight children in Timaru (New Zealand). Her parents were dirt-poor farmers, their lives straitened and unluxurious. Mary excelled at the one-teacher local school but there was nothing beyond the primary level. At the age of 13 she was looking after the home while her mother recovered from the death of twins. 'Nothing but work, work, all day long', she remembered afterwards.

She got a job as a domestic servant and nursemaid. Then like many bright country girls, she took up nursing. This brought her to Sydney, where she landed a job in the small hospital at Portland, a cement works and mining town over the western ranges. There she met Michael Ryan, also from a Catholic farming family.

In search of work, he had come to Portland as a teenager. An accident at the cement works cost him his leg at the age of 19. Given six weeks' pay and no further compensation, he found work in the local billiards saloon, in time becoming its proprietor. With two full-size tables, the billiards saloon, with the pubs, was one of the town's few social centres—men only of course.

After their marriage, the Ryans lived in a bare little cottage without electricity or running water. They had three children, of whom two would become teachers and the third a priest. Mrs Ryan was a reader. She got books from the local School of Arts and took out a subscription to the Left Book Club, which brought her a book a month from London.

She was a strong supporter of the nuns, black Josephites from Perthville. She pressed books on them and engaged them in conversation. When the ABC started its schools broadcasts, she saw how valuable they would be and made sure the parish school got the equipment to listen to them. Similarly, when later the nuns thought of trying to start a small secondary school, she encouraged them to go ahead and went to Sydney to find cheap desks for the school.

Mary Ryan was a faithful Catholic but she was not uncritical. One Sunday during World War II the priest at Mass attacked women for wanting kindergartens, saying such women were grossly selfish. The bishops were saying similar things then too. She went home and wrote an angry response in her journal. (Her journal, in 27 exercise books, will be an archive of grassroots Catholic history when it is published.)

By that time, Mary Ryan knew more about such things than the priest. In 1942 she had been a surprise appointment to the federal housing commission, a new body to tackle the shortage of homes. The minister was her good friend, Ben Chifley, who often called in to talk with her about politics. She was president of the local ALP branch and a delegate to state conferences of the Labor party. She was also a Justice of the Peace, who knew how tough life could be for the disadvantaged.

Nevertheless, when Chifley appointed her to the housing commission, there were murmurs of dissent from city women's organisations, who did not know her. She replied that she was a humble housewife who could speak with the authority of experience. She told a journalist, 'From my personal experience of bringing up a family in a little cottage with practically no conveniences, I know all about housekeeping disabilities and I think I know what women require'.

The war had highlighted Australia's need to increase its population. Dame Enid Lyons and Lady Cilento produced a report saying that the ideal family should have six children. The *Australian Women's Weekly* commented that it was not enough to exhort women to have larger families; they must have household amenities to make this easier. Mary Ryan agreed: 'Better housing should encourage an increase in the birthrate'. This agenda lay behind her work on the housing commission.

She also wanted to make women's lives more interesting. So she pressed hard for community centres in new housing estates. These would make available not only post-natal and childcare facilities but also cultural and social opportunities. If women weren't welcome in the pubs, they had to have meeting places of their own.

The postwar housing shortage put some of her ideas in the too-hard or the not-yet baskets. She didn't give up but kept raising a woman's voice in public forums. She stood for local government, earning the attention of an anti-Catholic newspaper, *The Rock*, who called her 'the red Mrs Ryan'. Crippled by arthritis and for her final three years bedridden, she remained, as one of her family said, an early non-ideological feminist.

Patriot and bookman

Fr LEO HAYES

FATHER LEO HAYES WROTE ALL HIS LETTERS with a fountain pen given to him by General Douglas Macarthur. When Macarthur came to Australia in 1942 to lead the war effort against Japan, detailed knowledge of the Pacific Islands and PNG was slight. Someone told the general about a Queensland bush priest who had a formidable collection of books and maps; so Macarthur asked Father Hayes for help. The American offered to pay for the heaps of valuable material the priest gave him but the bush PP wouldn't hear of it. Instead, he had dinner with the general, who presented him with a fountain pen.

For the next 25 years that pen was well used. Father Hayes was a great letter writer. He wrote to every child in the district who passed a public examination. He wrote congratulations on a birth, an engagement or a marriage. He wrote condolences on a death. When new stamps were issued, he sent first day covers to dozens of friends. In reply, he got seven or eight letters a day; and at Christmas, according to his curate's count, 600 cards.

This outgoing kindness marked his days in the parish. When he went to the cinema, he took lollies in his pockets to give to children. Each morning, collecting the mail, he would sit on the post office step talking to passers-by. He had a special liking for swaggies, going out of his way to engage them in conversation—thirty of them came to his funeral. The poet Mary Gilmore, a personal friend, said of him, 'If the sun shines on an act of kindness, it must always be shining on Father Leo Hayes'.

His friendship with poets like her was another side to his life. Hayes treasured Australian writers. His sermons and talks were spiced with allusions to Henry Kendall, John Shaw Nielson and 'Banjo' Paterson. Once, instead of a sermon, he read from the pulpit a Steele Rudd short story. Parishioners told him the 'sermon' had taught them how to pray.

Famously, Father Hayes collected Australian writers. The presbytery sank on its foundations under the weight of his collection. In the end, there were 25,000 books, pamphlets and periodicals and another 30,000 manuscript items, the originals of books, poems, lectures, radio plays and letters. There were maps, press clippings, stamps, postcards, pictures, as well as old guns, rocks, Aboriginal artefacts and cattle bells. The only things he didn't collect, said archivist Brother Leo Ansell, was antique furniture and machinery. On his death, all 25 tonnes of it went to the University of Queensland, where today it remains an unrivalled resource for scholars.

At the centre of the collection were the papers of A. G. Stephens, pioneer man of letters in Australian literature. Through the 'Red Page' of *The Bulletin*, his own magazine *The Bookfellow* and various publishing houses, Stephens had promoted the first generation of Australian nationalist writers, such as Paterson, Henry Lawson and Mary Gilmore. His papers, annotated in his trademark purple ink, are a unique archive of this period.

Alongside them Hayes put the books of the poets and fiction writers of Australia, often presented to him and autographed by their authors. He filled gaps in his collection by begging out-of-print books from friends. At the same time, he was generous with his own holdings.

A section specialised in Aboriginal lore. Wherever he served in the Toowoomba diocese, Hayes took care to collect vocabularies of the local languages, either from Aborigines themselves or from the records of pioneer settlers. Word collectors also handed over to him their own notebooks and vocabularies. These included *death wails*, 'the poignant expression of Aboriginal grief for their dead' as he called them.

This phrase comes from a 1941 article in *Manly*, the magazine of the priests who were ordained from the Manly seminary. Leo Hayes had been a star student in his seminary days, winning prizes for theology and public speaking. Never bashful about his ability to make a good speech, he would report accurately after a public occasion, 'I gave the best speech'.

Meeting fellow bibliophiles at the Sydney home of Walter Stone, he would enrich the occasion with a homiletic address. Some of his best remembered speeches were on Anzac Day and other national days. For like all the Manly men of his generation, he had absorbed with his theology a lively love of Australia, thus grafting patriotism on to Christian faith.

Scholar and mystic

Dr WILLIAM LEONARD

The obituaries did not tell the whole story when Dr William Leonard died in 1961. Of course they gave the external details of his life: birth in Ireland 69 years earlier, study in Rome, arrival as a young graduate at Manly seminary, where he lectured on the Bible and published biblical commentaries, then an exemplary death surrounded by colleagues and disciples as he made the responses himself to the prayers of the last rites.

The obituarists were shy of mentioning what was obvious to everyone who knew Dr Leonard, that he was a mystic. His mystical experience was most manifest on Fridays, when he became speechless and immobile. If mystical experience, as dictionaries say, is an apprehension of the divine, there can be little doubt that each Friday brought him to share in the Passion of Christ. On other days of the week, priests who celebrated Mass in the little chapel where he lived could not fail to notice him in a corner behind the door, rapt in another world.

In a nearby parish, where he took duty while the resident priest went on annual holidays, the housekeeper was amazed at the long hours he spent before the Blessed Sacrament.

This mystical experience gave fire and energy to his understanding of the Bible. To him it was not just a literary text awaiting scholarly elucidation, like Shakespeare or Homer—it was the Word of God, the breath of the Spirit, a portrait of someone he already knew well, the Lord himself. To him it really was a sacred text. He knew it in his heart before he knew it in his head.

This appreciation of the Bible demanded more, not less, scholarship. After a dozen years teaching at Manly, he went back to Rome and enrolled in the Pontifical Biblical Institute for a doctorate. The institute's doctorate of Sacred Scripture is one of the world's rarest degrees. It was no surprise, after World War II, that the English Catholic Biblical Association asked him to write the commentary on the Epistle to the Hebrews for its *Catholic Commentary on the Bible*. He also wrote the commentary on the Book of Ruth and some of the book's introductory essays. The Protestant historian Stuart Piggin calls him 'the architect of vital Australian Catholic Biblical scholarship'.

A former student, the historian Thomas McNevin Veech, said that to hear him on St John's Gospel was an unforgettable experience and that his lectures on the Passion were superb in scholarship and piety. Asked in what field Dr Leonard had excelled, Veech replied: 'At one time Pauline theology seemed to win; at another the gospels, particularly St John's Gospel; in the last years of his life the Old Testament, when everything connected with the Jewish people and their history became a constant source of interest to him, so that a scholarly Rabbi recently said that Dr Leonard had outstripped him in Jewish lore'.

Intensely Catholic, he nevertheless had an easy rapport with scholars of other traditions. At his death, one of them said that they looked on him as a father in God. He met them at meetings of the Fellowship for Biblical Studies, where study of the Bible became a foundation for later ecumenical understandings.

At the heart of Dr Leonard's scholarship was an astonishing grasp of languages. He encountered Hebrew first on a tombstone near his boyhood home, copied out the inscription and took it home to puzzle over. College studies gave him Latin and Greek, to which he added a facility in Italian, French and German. He was conversant with semitic languages but towards the end of his life regretted that he had not become a master in them, since they were often a key to Old Testament puzzles. Archbishop Simonds of Melbourne once said of him, 'He does his thinking in Greek'. But on his deathbed he spoke mainly in Latin, with some quotations in Greek.

For over twenty years this remarkable scholar devoted time to writing about the Bible for the *Catholic Weekly*. He thus tried to make his scholarship available to everyday Catholics in the parishes. Sometimes he seemed to be trying to pack a library into a single sentence. No matter, his readers persevered. Like him, they knew, as he once told the editor, that they needed infusions of biblical thought or they would be swamped by the naturalism all around them.

Priest to the broken people

Fr TOM DUNLEA

THE YOUNG PRIEST COULD HEAR A BOY SINGING in the early hours of the morning. He sounded no more than six years old, and yet from somewhere in the Surry Hills children's shelter his voice penetrated to the presbytery next door: 'I wish I had someone to love me; someone to call me their own'.

The priest was Tom Dunlea and he never forgot that early morning singer. The memory stayed with him through 14 years as a curate in various Sydney parishes, some of them the toughest. Then he was made parish priest of Sutherland on the southern fringe of the city, where he found a number of his Depression-hit parishioners living in caves and humpies. Riding a white horse, he brought them food and hope, even giving away his own boots and overcoat. Years later, someone said of him, 'If he had given away anything else, he would have been charged with indecent exposure'.

One day a dying mother made him promise to care for her youngest son. Father Dunlea took him into the presbytery, and soon other homeless boys joined them there. They moved to a bigger house but the numbers kept growing, until neighbours began to complain to the local council. So the priest put his boys on the road and took them into the nearby bush to set up tents. The newspapers loved it. Publicity led to a gift of eleven acres at Engadine, where 'Boys' Town' started in August 1940.

The idea came from a Hollywood movie of the same name, starring Spencer Tracy and Mickey Rooney. The settlement was to be run by the boys themselves, with the priest's oversight.

Father Dunlea had all the legendary charm of a Tipperary man and he won instant support for his town from sporting and media circles. The meat and baking industries helped him set up a trade school there. Each Sunday a carnival with trotting, cycling and midget car racing packed the Sydney Sports Ground. In the war years this was a welcome respite from the Sunday observance laws.

By now there were dozens of boys in residence and at the archbishop's suggestion the De La Salle Brothers agreed to lend a hand. In 1947 the founder resigned his parish and moved to Boys' Town.

He was developing work among alcoholics, something that had drawn him since his early days in the inner city. In association with psychiatrist Dr Sylvester Minogue and Archie McKinnon of the Darlinghurst reception house, he was moving towards the beginning of Alcoholics Anonymous in Australia. For a time the pioneer AA group met in the Boys' Town city office and other locations found by the priest.

Not all of his ideas were winners and some of his swans turned into geese. A bush camp for alcoholics and a residential, 'Christmas House', both failed , which seemed to prove that a controlled environment was not the answer to alcoholism.

Boys' Town fund-raising functions had sharpened the priest's own drinking problems and he came to recognise that he himself was an alcoholic. AA sources are justly reticent about their members' life stories, but one who knew him then says, 'He fixed up early ... he didn't do much damage'. From now on, when he stood up at AA meetings, he would begin with those humbly heroic words, 'I'm Father Tom and I'm an alcoholic'.

In 1950, he took a year's leave of absence to wander round Australia. On his return, he became chaplain to the Matthew Talbot Hostel for destitute men, where his listening kindness was given full stretch. Then he returned to parish work, devoting much time to AA and a new body for people with psychiatric problems, Recovery (today called GROW), as well as to a menagerie of odd animals. The menagerie is a significant clue to Father Tom's personality, his brimming-over concern for any part of creation that was in need. He once said, 'When Tom Dunlea doesn't take an interest in stray dogs any longer, you'll know that he's had it'. The Christmas crib outside his presbytery featured a real lamb, a goat, pigeons, a donkey and a kangaroo.

Although technically he was parish priest of Hurstville in the archdiocese of Sydney, in reality his parish was Australia-wide, for he felt called wherever there were broken people. 'No priest', Cardinal Gilroy said, 'has done more to make the church loved.' At his death in 1970, the congregation around his grave at Boys' Town included a pet sheep and a stray dog.

A champion
for girls

JULIA FLYNN

WHEN JULIA FLYNN BECAME THE CHIEF INSPECTOR of Victorian secondary schools in 1928, her friends rejoiced. It was the highest post ever held by a woman in the state's public service. Her previous positions, as assistant and then as acting chief inspector, had also made her the current top woman in the public service. The chief inspectorship, however, was the real thing — a moment for joy and con-`gratulations.

There were qualifications to their joy. Her salary, for instance, was four-fifths of the male rate. Unimaginable today, this was the convention of the time, which was resented by women like Julia Flynn. There were other sour notes in their memories. When the assistant chief inspector's job had fallen vacant, the words of the advertisement seemed to imply that it was open only to men. Julia protested; and won the position. Within months the chief inspector's job was vacant, only this time the advertisement was specific. *Male Required*, it stated.

This seemed to contravene recent legislation outlawing discrimination against women for being female or married. The director of education took responsibility for the advertisement. 'A woman could not do the work', he said. Outraged women peppered the newspapers with letters. Women's clubs and organisations protested publicly. *The Age* attacked the advertisement as a mistake. Still, the director of education stood firm. He told the minister for education that the majority of schoolgirls would become housewives; that secondary schools were mainly for boys; and this made it unsuitable to appoint a woman as chief inspector; indeed, he had worded the advertisement in such a way as to stop Julia Flynn.

In the face of public outcry, the minister overruled his education director and the position was readvertised. Julia Flynn put her name in…and lost. The winner was a former Rhodes Scholar with a fine academic and professional record who would one day become director of education. Nevertheless, he was in several ways junior to Julia Flynn and she, exercising her right of appeal, took the case to the public service commissioner. He upheld her appeal. So she got the position at last.

But not for long. The education director did not accept his defeat by the public service commissioner. He knew that senior posts were held on probation; and after six months' probation he announced that he would not confirm Julia's appointment. So the Rhodes Scholar got the job and Julia Flynn went back to being an assistant chief inspector. By the time she got the top job again, there were other women at an equal grade in the public service.

The downgrading of Julia Flynn had some bitter ironies. She was a pioneer Catholic feminist who actively worked for women's equality in the workforce and at home. One of the founders of the Catholic Women's Social Guild, she served on its inaugural committee. The guild stood for equal pay (not four-fifths) for women and for equity at work. When St Joan's Alliance, an activist political group of Catholic women, started in Melbourne, she was one of its first members.

As well, there had been a feminist tendency in her work. She did not think that quality education should be reserved for boys' schools and worked hard to bring girls' domestic science schools into the educational mainstream. In particular, she objected to 'little girls of 12 and 13 spending more than half of their school time in cooking, washing, ironing and scrubbing to the sacrifice of their general education and health'. She had also tried to introduce music and creative arts into secondary schools.

As a retiree, she spent the last five years of her life advising Catholic schools in Victoria. She suggested that nuns and brothers attend university full-time, not after a day in the classrooms. She wanted specialist art teachers alongside the music teachers who had made Catholic schools famous for their music. She thought the curriculum in girls' schools was too narrow and that everyone paid too much attention to scoring well in examinations.

The Christian Brothers would not let her into their schools and few of the others paid much attention to her advice. When she died, the people she had tried to help established an annual prize in her memory. All her life she had criticised the obsession with high examination marks. In a final irony, her memorial prize went to the pupil from a Catholic school who gained highest marks in the external matriculation exams.

A Renaissance man

Br GEORGE COLUMBA DAVY

WHEN BROTHER GEORGE COLUMBA DAVY went to afternoon tea with Patrick White in 1964, what struck him about the author's home were the paintings. There were three Sidney Nolans, who was already internationally known and at that time a close friend of White. As well as Nolan, a gallery of lesser-known Australian artists crowded the walls. Brother Davy noticed Roy de Maistre, Dickerson, Gleghorn, Coburn, Gleeson, Perceval and Fairweather. In the back garden there was a metal sculpture by Clement Meadmore.

Reading the account Davy wrote about his afternoon tea with White, one is struck by how unusual this Christian Brother must have been. Without disrespect, one may guess that there were few brothers at that time who could have recognised or discussed painters then at the cutting edge of Australian art.

His mother died when he was four. His father, a veteran of

Gallipoli and the war in France, sent him to live with a child-less couple on Flinders Island in South Australia. They were the only residents on the island and the little boy was with them for two years. Back in Adelaide, he was noticed by a St Vincent de Paul man and his wife and sent to Rostrevor College. From there, at the age of 14, he came to the Christian Brothers.

An early appointment was to the Sydney harbourside par-ish school at Rose Bay. The suburb is a real estate agent's dream but for the Christian Brothers it was more like a night-mare. Four or five brothers shared a cottage next to the school. With only two bedrooms available in the cottage, three of the brothers camped in the school basement; and when that was needed, they moved into the so-called community room, where there was not even space for wardrobes. Rain leaked into the superior's bedroom; so when he fell ill one winter, he moved his bedding onto the community table. One of the school mothers accidentally discovered him there and the subsequent row in the parish ensured better living quarters for the brothers. Even in Rose Bay, the Christian Brothers were true to form: they taught the sons of the poor and lived in poverty themselves.

Rose Bay was the making of G. C. Davy. With a recent arts degree from Melbourne University (studying at night, of course), he was put in charge of the humanities side of the senior school. They were small classes, so boys and teacher formed bonds which lasted for life: half a century after their schooldays they still spoke of him affectionately. He put prints of Raphael and Dobell on the walls and introduced the boys to Beethoven and Tchaikovsky through record evenings. He ran the literary and debating society and brought in guest speak-ers. He even found time for the cadet corps.

In 1959 he was sent to the teacher training college at

Strathfield (NSW) to be master of Christian Brother scholastics. The next year his landmark *The Christian Gentleman* was published. The subtitle announced it as a book of courtesy and social guidance for boys and it was to become a textbook in Christian Brothers' colleges. Davy knew that boys are not born with good manners, any more than they are born with a good prose style; but each can be acquired. Without care in the schools, the Australian democratic temper could produce boors or hillbillies. His book was a counterweight to this tendency.

His fourteen years at Strathfield can be assessed in various ways. Historians of education recall his innovations in encouraging future teachers to learn by doing: the microteaching rooms; the one-way mirrors between demonstration classes and an observation room; and the videotaping of practice lessons. He also made it easier for scholastics to get university degrees.

Church historians recall his decade as editor of the Christian Brothers' *Our Studies* magazine before and after Vatican II. In those champagne years he reminded his readers that yesterday's theology would not meet tomorrow's problems.

Most of all, those who knew G. C. Davy would agree with his obituarist in *Our Studies*, that to him emotion and spirit were as important as intellect and theory. For those whom he educated, he was a Renaissance man who had fitted them wonderfully for life. As one of them said in a poem: others built buildings; he built men—by introducing them to master spirits like Benjamin Britten, Hopkins, Degas, Rouault and Patrick White.

Publishers to Vatican II

SUE & GEOFFREY CHAPMAN

THE YEARS PRECEDING THE SECOND VATICAN COUNCIL (1962-65) are beginning to attract the attention of historians. They realise that the great council, which effected so much change in the life of the church, did not happen out of the blue. Rather, the bishops in council ratified changes that were already on the way. For decades before it, writers and thinkers, lay leaders and ecclesiastics had tested the ideas which came to fruition in Vatican II.

One of the test-beds of such ideas in Australia was Melbourne University. From 1950, commonwealth scholarships, a Menzies government initiative, had opened the universities to more young Catholics than had previously been able to pursue a degree. Vast numbers of these university men and women would move into the professions, thus changing the socio-economic makeup of Australian Catholicism.

As well, they would introduce into Catholicism ideas and

principles acquired at university, such as the liberal principle of free speech. The Catholicism they experienced at university was in some ways different from that of the parishes. Clergy and laity were closer together, so that there was a ready acceptance of lay leadership. Ecumenism, biblical spirituality, congregational liturgy, openness to Australian culture—such were the waves of the future already being experienced in lay apostolate groups at university.

Geoffrey Chapman and Sue James were products of the lay apostolate at Melbourne University. Daughter of an old Tasmanian family, she was a student of English literature. He had been under the influence of the Jesuits since going to Kostka Hall at the age of seven. Then came Xavier, where he was chiefly distinguished at rowing. Enrolled as a law student, he spent part of his university years at Newman College.

It was, however, the Newman Society and that genial Jesuit Fr Jerry Golden, who changed their lives. They became committed lay Catholics, eager to put their talents at the service of the Kingdom. In 1953 they co-authored an article in the *Melbourne University Magazine* about the spiritual gaps in university life. Some months later they married in Newman College chapel and within a week set sail for London.

The Melbourne University apostolate grew from the ideas of a Belgian priest, Joseph Cardijn. Cardijn's Young Christian Workers (YCW) movement had become the outstanding twentieth century exemplar of a lay movement, and the Newman Society adapted its insights to local conditions. So as soon as they had settled in London, the Chapmans went looking for the YCW. While Geoffrey worked as a lawyer and later as a school teacher, much of their free time was spent in YCW circles.

Sitting in their kitchen one night with YCW president Pat Keegan and chaplain Fr Edward Mitchison, the Chapmans offered to edit a book on the movement. That project fell through but it led to another, a collection of talks by Joseph Cardijn. Then came a second book, the writings of Cardinal Suhard, archbishop of Paris, whose visionary pastoral letters influenced radically that generation of Catholics. The Chapmans had found what they wanted to do with their lives; they would become publishers.

Borrowing money, Geoffrey went to Chicago for three months, working at Fides Publishers. 'He fell on the tremendous generosity of the Americans', his wife said later. 'They fed him, lodged him, encouraged and gave help, ideas, information and friendship.'

That friendship stood by them in years to come. When, in February 1957, Geoffrey Chapman Ltd, Publishers, was set up, its first book was Leo Trese's *Many Are One*, a Fides title. Over the years they would publish each other's books, on both sides of the Atlantic.

The Chapmans remembered their debt to the Melbourne apostolate too, by publishing an international edition of Melbourne talks, *The Incarnation in the University*. Many of their earliest books were translations of French writers: Masure, Montcheuil, Doncoeur, Guitton, Hasseveldt, Loew and Richaud. They were part of the postwar reawakening which led towards Vatican II.

So the firm of Geoffrey Chapman was well placed to meet the challenges of the council. Young Catholics eager to join in the updating of Catholicism joined the staff. They knew what the key ideas would be and found writers who were able to explore them. When the council documents appeared in English with expert commentaries (including one on priests by Hobart's Archbishop Young), it seemed right that the publisher was Geoffrey Chapman. For by then the Chapmans' firm, more than any other in the English-speaking world, could be called the authentic publishers to Vatican II.

A lover
of art

Fʀ MICHAEL SCOTT

Wʜᴇɴ ᴀʀᴄʜɪᴛᴇᴄᴛ Jᴏʜɴ Mᴏᴄᴋʀɪᴅɢᴇ ᴡᴏɴ ᴛʜᴇ ᴄᴏɴᴛʀᴀᴄᴛ to design a Melbourne parish church, he thought it an opportunity to put some good religious art there. He persuaded the parish priest to commission a triptych from Sydney artist Justin O'Brien. O'Brien seemed a good choice. A decade earlier, in 1951, he had won the inaugural Blake Prize for Religious Art with a triptych, *The Virgin Enthroned*, which the National Gallery of Victoria had acquired.

It was ironical, perhaps, that the inaugural winner of the Blake Prize should find a home in the Melbourne gallery, because the Blake Prize aimed to put art in churches rather than in galleries. What it wanted was sacred art, that is, art for liturgical use. Its inspiration was the French sacred art movement which had won the collaboration of the best modern artists and brought the church and modern art together. Why couldn't the same happen here? Such were the hopes of a cultivated Jesuit, Michael Scott, who with a Jewish businessman friend founded the annual Blake Prize to further these hopes.

Happily, just as the Melbourne church commission for Justin O'Brien was going ahead, Father Scott came to Melbourne to be rector of Newman College at Melbourne University. He knew O'Brien's work well from his days as the first headmaster of the Sydney preparatory school, Campion Hall. O'Brien's religious sense, he wrote, 'seeps through slowly to the viewer who has the patience to stand before it and wait for it to speak, but when it does start to speak there is almost no end to the song'. Now, in Melbourne, an O'Brien work was actually being commissioned for a new Catholic church. After ten years the hopes of the Blake Prize founder were being fulfilled.

When the new triptych arrived it proved to be a stronger painting than *The Virgin Enthroned*. Placed above the altar of the Lady Chapel in the new church, it quickly attracted peoples' devotion. But the parish priest, all powerful in these matters, wasn't happy. He began to have doubts. Were the Virgin Mary's legs in the Annunciation panel too pronounced? Were the wings of the angels of the enthronement too bright? Was Elizabeth at the Visitation too young? He went into town, bought something at Pellegrini's and put it on the Lady Chapel wall instead of Justin O'Brien's triptych.

For Michael Scott and the sacred art movement it was a dispiriting defeat. The rector of Newman College bought the rejected triptych for a cut price and added it to the college collection, where today it is one of the treasures.

There was another defeat at the same time. Father Scott had collaborated with a small publisher in bringing out a religious art calendar for 1963. The calendar lost money and Scott advised the publisher to cut up the remaining stock for marketing as prints or postcards. There would be no Michael Scott religious art calendar for 1964.

Even the Blake Prize seemed under threat. In 1961 Stanislaus Rapotec had won the prize with a huge abstract painting called *Meditating on Good Friday*. Scott disagreed with the decision and said so publicly. He would not call a painting religious if it lacked any obvious pictorial references to religion. The dispute came down to the question: What is religious art? A majority of the judges decided, in effect, that a painting was religious if the artist said so. For the sacred art movement it was a parting of the ways. In 1962 Robert Hughes, a youthful participant in the debate who would later become *Time* magazine's art critic, mocked Scott's sacred art hopes: 'Is it not significant how few modern works of art have crept into our churches over the last ten years, despite the Blake Prize?'

Michael Scott remained at Newman College until 1968. Then he left the Jesuits, went overseas and, in time, moved to Dublin and married the fiction writer Mary Lavin, a contemporary at university. He left behind at Newman a marvellous collection of contemporary Australian art. It reveals the breadth of his tastes, the friendships he shared with some fine artists and his own willingness to grow (for there is abstract work there).

At Newman College too there is an evocative monument to his vision. It is the tiny oratory next to the college hall, which he created in partnership with Victorian artists. The oratory's clean lines and local artefacts recall Michael Scott's hopes that the Australian church would find a way of praying liturgically in the authentic accents of our own culture.

Training for a different race

HERB ELLIOTT

HERB ELLIOTT IS IN EVERYONE'S TOP TEN of Australian sportsmen. His win in the 1500 metres race at the 1960 Olympic Games, is a landmark in Australian athletics. Seventeen times he broke the four-minute mile. His pinnacle performances as a runner continue to inspire young athletes. From him they learn that there is more to gold medal running than physical fitness.

A schoolboy champion at Aquinas College, Perth, Herb Elliott caught the attention of eastern state officials. Coach Percy Cerutty told him he could be a world-beater in two years. But, moving a piano for a school dance, he broke his foot, and as parties and the beach beckoned, he lost interest in athletics.

Worried that their son was at a loose end, his parents timed a family visit to Melbourne to coincide with the Olympic Games of 1956. That brush with glory re-lit his interest in running. He persuaded his parents to allow him to stay in Melbourne so that he could train with Percy Cerutty. A tough coach,

Cerutty put his charges through punishing runs in the Portsea sandhills and long fitness routines in the gymnasium. At the same time, he insisted that inner attitude was the secret to running well. 'Percy helped me to world records', said Elliott. 'Not so much by improving my technique, but by releasing in my mind and soul a power that I only vaguely thought existed.'

Like the founder of the modern Olympic movement, Baron de Coubertin, Elliott sees sport in moral terms. To succeed, one must push oneself beyond the comfort zone. 'There is a degree of self-mastery in all of this, a bit of discipline, some self-control. There are important steps in allowing our spirit to grow in us rather than see it drown in self-indulgence.'

Watching the Russian sailor Vladimir Kuts triumph in his long distance races at the Melbourne Games excited Elliott and made him eager to win Olympic gold too. Training, however, was the time when such enthusiasm was put to the test, to see if it was more than a flash in the pan. Training was lonely, often in dull or brutal environments. Slow down, cried his body, let up. No, no, said his spirit, these are the moments which will decide whether you will win at the Olympics. 'It was always the spirit, that part of me that is both inside me and separate from the body, that became the strength; that ignored the tired compromise and just got on with it. Don't tell me that sport isn't spiritual.'

And so he trained and ran and broke records and went to Rome to represent Australia at the 1960 Olympics. All the time his intense focus was on himself. Even when he put on the Australian kit in Rome he felt he was running for himself. Then he won—by the extraordinary margin of 20 metres. When they played the national anthem and unfurled the Australian flag as he received his gold medal, he felt an intense burst of patriotism. His previous focus had been within; now he knew he belonged also to his fellow Australians. His eyes filled with tears and he realised that he had learnt something new that day.

Herb Elliott went on learning, went on growing. All his life he has remained close to athletics. Today he is a senior statesman of the Olympic movement. Recent Olympic Games have seen him appointed as stress adviser to Australian teams. His job is to counsel athletes how to handle the stress of media attention, sudden success or defeat. When Debbie Flintoff-King won the 400 metres hurdles race at the Seoul Games in 1988, setting a new Olympic record, she was carrying an inspirational message from Elliott.

Religiously, Percy Cerutty was a sceptic. His dominating personality could unsettle young people. For a time Elliott became a bit wobbly in his faith, although he was never satisfied with mere scepticism. In Rome, however, faith came back to him. There, he said, 'I leant on my religion heavily'.

In an interview with *Australian Catholics* magazine the mature Elliott said he was going deeper into religion. Stirred by Marriage Encounter, he now meditatds and read for an hour each day.

Still committed to the church ('Catholicism is my tradition—I've been a Catholic for 55 years and I'll be one for the rest of my life'), he delights in fresh insights from other spiritualities. So the great runner is still in training ... only it is for a different race.

The challenge and opportunity of service

Dame ROMA MITCHELL

To CELEBRATE THEIR 150TH ANNIVERSARY in 1986, South Australians put plaques along Adelaide's North Terrace, commemorating men and women who had made SA history. One of the plaques reads:

> DAME ROMA MITCHELL OBE
> Born 1913
> Jurist, first woman QC in Australia

If they ever update that plaque, they will add the fact that in 1991 Dame Roma Mitchell became Governor of South Australia, the first woman to become an Australian state governor.

She was a popular choice because her work as a lawyer had won many people's affections. Among her early clients were women who were victims of domestic violence. 'I've acted for women who couldn't leave a drunken, violent husband because they had young children,' she once said. 'He owned the house, nobody could order him to get out. There were no women's shelters and no pensions. It was a pretty tough state of affairs in those days.'

The Great Depression made a deep impression on her too. All her life she has remembered the long queue of men in Kintore Avenue waiting for their dole tickets. Close to where she worked as an articled clerk she would see each day men lining up to get a few shillings from the proprietor of the *Advertiser*.

Her sister, a journalist, wrote Depression-slanted articles, such as how to make children's clothes out of wheat bags. It is no surprise, then, to find that as a mature jurist, Dame Roma served for eight years as chair of the Parole Board and another five years as Chair of the Human Rights Commission.

Reviewing a book of Catholic history, Dr George Shaw has said that a characteristic of Catholics in Australian history has been their passion for justice. Anyone wishing to follow up Shaw's insight might find evidence in Dame Roma Mitchell's story. The parish priest where she grew up, Fr Cornelius Crowley, was a legendary friend of the battlers. He always looked underdressed because he gave away his clothes to those in greater need.

Once he arrived for Sunday mass in bare feet: he had given his shoes to a swagman on the road. Another time, visiting the Mitchell house in midwinter, he was asked by Mrs Mitchell what had happened to his nice overcoat. Oh, a poor fellow had come to the presbytery and he needed it more than the priest. His was a powerful influence on the growing girl.

There were negative influences too. South Australian Catholics, being only 16 per cent of the population, long felt themselves to be outsiders. There were places where they were unwelcome, such as banks and certain business firms. Young Roma felt this. A brilliant student at the Angas Street Mercy convent, she had topped the state in Latin and elected to study Law.

Her war widow mother took her to a solicitor to arrange for her to become an articled clerk. What is your religion, he asked her. I don't think that's a proper question to ask, replied the mother. After that, they had to find another firm to take her on.

It wasn't all one way, of course. Looking across the great Reformation divide, Catholics were defensive in ways that others found to be offensive. Roma's father was a low church Anglican who resented being married in the sacristy without full ceremonial. At the university, when a popular student died, Catholic office holders in the Law Students' Society could not act as pallbearers. They felt that keenly. Catholics had their own body at the university, the Aquinas Society, of which Roma was women's president. Her connections with Adelaide University were lifelong. In 1983 she became its Chancellor, the first woman to be a university chancellor in Australia.

One of the groups working towards better days was the Catholic Women's League. As described by Margaret Press in her history of South Australian Catholics, it was never sectarian or inward looking. Roma Mitchell was its legal adviser and a frequent speaker at its conferences. Recently she recalled, 'they were not confined to Catholic matters and always joined in everything that was important in a social sense'.

On Ash Wednesday 1992, an interstate journalist went to early morning Mass at the cathedral and was surprised to see the governor sitting quietly on her own. No aide-de-camp, no driver—as usual, she had walked through the city to Mass. The priest came out looking for someone to do the readings and lit on Her Excellency, who did the job without fuss. The journalist reflected that although she had risen high in the world, Dame Roma Mitchell had never gone far from her Catholic roots.

Dedicated to migrants

FR ALDO LORIGIOLA

THE SCALABRINI FATHERS WERE FOUNDED a century ago to give pastoral care to Italian emigrants. So it made sense for the Bishop of Wollongong to invite them to Australia in the 1950s. Wollongong is a centre of heavy industry which then employed thousands of young Italian males, who felt out of place in the average parish.

Among the Scalabrinians was the 25-year-old Aldo Lorigiola. Handsome, zealous and a good organiser, he plunged into the work. Old Australian parishioners, who had not yet learned to live in a multicultural society, did not always appreciate his enthusiasm for inviting all Italians in the district to come to their church. With some courage, the young priest preached about racism. In time, the parishioners got used to Italians, or went elsewhere. Pretty soon half the weddings in their church were all-Italian ceremonies.

Meanwhile the priests could see that these new settlers

needed a place of their own. Using money given by American friends, Lorigiola bought an old house in the centre of Wollongong and transformed it into a migrants' centre. He used volunteer labour, so the people who came to the centre felt it was their own, not just another social service provided by authorities. Here they learned English, made friends, went to dances and found a chapel and priests attentive to their own religious culture.

Four years later Lorigiola was sent to Melbourne, to work in the new Scalabrinian parish of Fitzroy. Again he was keen to involve the laity in the mission of the church. This led to the formation of a Catholic Action body, the Italian Catholic Federation, in 1960. ICF members were a picked force who were not only part of the Scalabrinian outreach to Italian migrants but also an attempt to develop lay leadership within the Italo-Australian community.

The ICF spread from Fitzroy to other Scalabrinian parishes and soon had hundreds of members. They found the atmosphere more open than the tight Catholicism they had known in parishes back in Italy. In the ICF the buzz-words were dialogue, cooperation and freedom to express your faith through work and commitment to others.

Not that Father Lorigiola was without critics. The Capuchin paper *La Fiamma* attacked him for empire-building. To start the ICF he had taken over an earlier Italian body which had connections with the Santamaria political movement: more criticism. It must be said that the priest invited criticism by his bossy clericalism—he treated the organisation he had founded as his own, an attitude which in those Vatican II years clashed with a growing desire for lay autonomy.

But he rode out all criticism, thanks to his superb ability to charm his followers. The historian of the ICF, Ivano Ercole, says that once he had gathered an audience the rest was easy.

His skilful eloquence and contagious enthusiasm, even when he was in sceptical or hostile surroundings, rarely failed to convince.

Then he was made Australian provincial of the Scalabrinians. Here his commitment to the ICF became a top priority. The new provincial expected every one of his priests to accept it also as a priority. Those who did not share his enthusiasm were soon in trouble, demoted or sent to hard assignments. Still in his thirties, perhaps he was too unseasoned for provincial leadership. In any case, dissident voices were now heard among the Scalabrinians.

He himself seemed to become more hesitant and less self-confident. Clever literary detective work by Ivano Ercole on Lorigiola's writings in the ICF magazine has revealed some unease about clerical celibacy.

In 1967 he refused a further appointment as provincial, went back to Italy and applied there for laicisation from the priesthood. Later he would tell author Desmond O'Grady that he left with $26.00 in his pocket. He picked up a quickie degree at a church university and landed a job at Padua university. Then he sent for a girl he had known in the ICF and married her.

Aldo Lorigiola's story did not end there. In the north of Italy there were thousands of returnees from Australia who kept alive a warm regard for their sometime country of adoption. Lorigiola helped organise them into an association of ex-emigrants, of which he became the president. Today the association has a magazine (*Il Canguro—The Kangaroo*); it has regular reunions and holiday trips back to Australia and lobbies governments for its members. So its founder-president is still fulfilling his original vocation, caring for migrants.

The heart of
the matter

Dr HARRY WINDSOR

THE TAXI STOPPED OUTSIDE ST MARY'S CATHEDRAL, Sydney, a man got out and went inside. After a few minutes he emerged and got into the taxi again. The taxi took him to St Vincent's Hospital, where he performed Australia's first heart transplant. The date was 23 October 1968. The man was Dr Harry Windsor.

Dr Windsor's visit to the cathedral, to pray before the climax of his career, was of a piece with his life. He was a believing, careful Catholic-whose life was rooted in faith.

A Brisbane boy, he was educated by the Christian Brothers at Gregory Terrace and Nudgee. They gave him a lifelong love of rugby as well as that manly Catholicism which is their trademark and which is very real, however matter-of-fact it may appear.

From his father, a general practitioner, he learnt some of the most important lessons about medicine long before he got to medical school. He often went with his father on house calls at night. Sitting in the car, waiting, taught him about the long hours of discipline, sacrifice and concern that were all part of the medical life.

Another key influence was Archbishop James Duhig, a family friend for 50 years. The Windsor family still tell wonderful stories about the lovable archbishop of Brisbane whose door was never closed to those in need. The Windsors also observed the human quirks of the great man, which saved them from any syrupy adulation of the clergy.

Equally, when Harry Windsor himself became a doctor at St Vincent's Hospital, he came to value highly the Sisters of Charity there, without idealising them. He could tell many stories about characters in the convent, such as the feminist Sister Hilarion, who liked to dissect the selfishness of men. 'Even in the Holy Family', she would say, 'the Virgin carries the Child, St Joseph holds the lilies.'

St Vincent's, the oldest Catholic hospital in Australia, became Harry Windsor's home ground. 'I regarded the day I took up my appointment at St Vincent's as the day I began my life's work', he wrote.

In preparation for that work, he spent two and a half years doing postgraduate study in England. These were lonely years, for he could not afford to take his wife Mollie and their young family with him. More than most people realise, the wives and children of famous doctors share in their medical successes.

And so, for better or for worse, this was the man who came to St Vincent's. Along with others he pioneered chest surgery there. That first heart transplant operation received Australia-wide publicity. Behind it, unnoticed by the public, was a lifetime of medical devotion.

One of his patients was the poet Elizabeth Riddell. Many years later she recalled the impact he made on her when she went to have a cancerous lung removed: 'I was amazed at the man—his authority, straight-forwardness, a kind of stillness. Even his good looks were somehow reassuring'.

Harry Windsor regarded his patients as people who paid him the compliment of asking for his help. The trust and confidence of that cry for help was the basis of the bond between them. Somehow his patients got to hear that he used to pray for them regularly in his parish church—that helped their confidence, too.

Then came the day when the great surgeon became a patient himself. One look at the X-ray told him that he had cancer. During his final illness, colleagues encouraged him to write his memoirs. So *The Heart of a Surgeon*, dedicated to four of the St Vincent's nuns, was published a few months after his death.

It is a profound, wise book, yet easy to read. A book about a doctor's life for those who have never been inside a medical school. A book about growing up as an Australian Catholic and living as an Australian Catholic. Most of all, it is about medicine as a vocation—in the way one used to speak about a vocation to the religious life or to the priesthood. Dr Windsor calls one of his chapters 'The Privilege of Working'. That says it all.

A distant vision

MASLYN WILLIAMS

WHEN MASLYN WILLIAMS ARRIVED IN AUSTRALIA in 1928, aged 17, a kindly gentleman took him on a tour of Sydney. Standing at the South Head of the harbour and pointing out to the Pacific Ocean, his guide said something that would give purpose to Maslyn's life:

'This is where Australia's influence and future lies, not in Europe or America, but within this area stretching from Antarctica, right through the Pacific, and so on into Asia. Here it must take its connections, establish allies, make friends and create relationships. What a monumental task is waiting for people of your age and the next generations of Australians.'

Never forgotten, those words challenged Maslyn Williams throughout his life. The son of an English soldier and an Australian mother, he came to his mother's country after both parents had died. In reference books he appears as 'former jackeroo, seaman, gold prospector, music student, war correspondent (film)'. A disparate life, you might guess, one full of experience for a future writer.

He first made his name in the burgeoning film industry of the 1930s, working as an editor mixing music and dialogue. On the outbreak of war he became producer-writer with the Australian war film unit. For five years he reported the war in North Africa, Greece, Crete and Syria, with forays into Ethiopia and Iraq.

The legendary war cameraman, Damien Parer, became a close friend and they wrote to each other weekly. The two film enthusiasts shared a deep commitment to the Catholic faith. When Parer died, Williams said something that has been repeated in everything subsequently written about him:

'When Damien did all that scrupulous work on his cameras, preparing them as a priest might the chalice, he wasn't doing it for himself, but for God. His faith was limitless.'

Postwar film-making included a stint with the Canadian Film Board and a year in Germany in the refugee camps. Back in Australia, Maslyn's abiding love of music drew him to the national music camps and the Australian Youth Orchestra, where he became friends with Monsignor Percy Jones. His films began to collect awards: first prize in Venice for a children's film; a UNESCO award for a film on music; and later a special award for the best film at the Melbourne 1900-1950 retrospective film festival.

In the 1950s Paul Hasluck, as Minister for Territories, asked him to go to Papua New Guinea to make films. His was a double charge: to record on film people whom many regarded as survivors of the Stone Age; and to make films which would be for them a crash course in modern civilisation. His films were the first to be admitted as evidence to the UN Trusteeship Council.

From this experience came his first book, prompted by his friend Morris West. *Stone Age Island* (1964) was followed two years later by a book on Indonesia, then books on China, Cambodia, the Philippines, Japan and Korea. These were travel books with a serious purpose. They did not waste space with the usual travellers' tips on where to eat or what to see. Instead, they concentrated on unfolding for an Australian audience the realities of life in the north.

Maslyn Williams writes his books with a film-maker's skill. He cuts from scene to scene, compressing each one as though it were seen through a camera lens. His writing also includes fiction, and he has published four novels.

The books are courteous and sympathetic in their willingness to learn from other cultures. In a letter written on his way to Indonesia in 1965, Williams said he was going there because he thought some enduring truths about human continuity might have survived there. 'We of the West lost the track at the time of the Industrial Revolution.' By going back and joining our neighbours on common ground, he said, we might pick up that lost track and go onwards together.

In the past 50 years Australians have been learning how to live in our own region, in this post-colonial world. Maslyn Williams wrote in the epilogue to *Faces of My Neighbour* (1979): 'History has now put the finger on us and we must set about earning a place for ourselves in a contemporary context—which means in this region'. His books have been a valuable part of that learning experience.

Acting by word and deed

LENA GUSTIN

THIS IS THE STORY OF A WOMAN WHO HELPED TO CHANGE the way we live. The most important event in Australian society after the gold rushes has been the immigration boom that followed the Second World War. Once, Australia was a tight Anglo-Celtic society, settled in its ways and very British. Now, it is diverse in its style of dress, eating habits, cultural opportunities and even ways of speaking. The hundreds of thousands of migrants who came here from non-Anglo-Celtic lands have changed our world and made our lives richer.

There was a price to pay for this. Not everyone likes change and new ways can be destabilising. For the new settlers there was the pain of losing their fatherland, their native language and culture. So many things in Australia were novel that they often felt lonely and afraid.

Lena Gustin was like that when she came here from Italy in 1956 with her husband and two small children. She could not understand what people said to her in the shops. The food was strange and unattractive. Even the Catholicism she found here seemed different from what she had known back home, a communal and festive religion.

Then one day she found a suburban coffee shop that had just bought an espresso coffee machine—only the owner didn't know how to work it. She showed him how and he offered her a job. That was the start of things for Lena Gustin. Work put her in touch with many unfamiliar aspects of Australian society and began the process of making her feel at home.

Along the way she had met Evasio Costanzo, a migrant journalist then editing the weekly *La Fiamma*. Run by the Capuchin Fathers, the paper was part of their remarkable work in caring for Italian newcomers. Editor Costanzo quickly realised Lena Gustin's quality and he asked her to write for him.

For seven years she answered readers' queries about family problems and about the difficulties of settling in a new country. Eventually she was handling three pages of *La Fiamma* each week. Her writings became a chain linking a wide network of people who shared their experiencee of this new land. It countered the anonymity and isolation of Australian life, which magnified ordinary family problems.

Lena kept worrying about that Australian anonymity and isolation—there had to be other ways to beat it. So when the Capuchins offered her an Italian-language program on the Sydney Catholic radio station, 2SM, she readily accepted. Lena wanted something more immediate than that, however, and she found it at the Council of Churches' station, 2CH.

Her live-to-air program *Arrivederci Roma*, initially sponsored by the Capuchin Fathers, blossomed into a major item in 2CH's schedule. It was a mixture of news from home, Italian music and Lena's comments on her listeners' problems. Before long, bags and bags of mail began to arrive at the station for her. By the end of the 1960s she was reaching an audience of 300,000 and 2CH was devoting 12 per cent of its airtime to multilingual programs. When she transferred to another station in 1973, she took her listeners with her.

By now she was known universally as 'Mama Lena', an understanding, intelligent, sympathetic radio mother who spoke from the heart and to the heart. She could touch her listeners' pockets too, whether it was for a national disaster such as a flood or an earthquake back in Italy or for a personal need here in Australia. This side of her work became known as *Sorella Radio* (Sister Radio). It has been institutionalised in the Sorella Radio Welfare Fund and the Sorella Radio Infants' Home, of which she is still president. Both Italian and Australian governments honoured her.

In her broadcasting and journalism Lena Gustin made two things clear to Italian-Australians. The first was that they must remain true to their origins, proud of being Italian. The second was that they must learn to appreciate what Australia had to offer. When people lost heart and told her they were going back to Italy, she would reply, 'Make sure you get a re-entry visa to Australia—you'll be back'.

Today's Australia is very different from when she started work. The 750,000 strong Italian community is a valued part of our national life. Using her talents wisely and generously, Lena Gustin helped make this happen.

The new catechisms

Mgr JOHN F. KELLY

When Pope John Paul II gave the world his new catechism in 1992, he said he did it to encourage local churches to make their own catechisms. The faith might be eternal but it had to be expressed in here-and-now languages and cultures. The pope's wish was in line with the law of the Incarnation: in every age Christianity is voiced in local accents and idioms, expressing itself in the culture of its own time.

On reading the pope's letter, historians remembered that 30 years earlier a series of Australian catechisms had done just that. Commissioned by the bishops, these new books took into account the people who would use them. The students of those days were more interactive than those of the past; they wanted religious teaching related to their own experience; they expected to 'make' religion rather than just learn about it.

By then, there was considerable disquiet about the teaching of religion in schools. For 80 years Australian Catholics had been brought up on a standard small book of questions and answers, the 'penny' catechism. It emphasised rote learning, obligation and linguistic precision rather than intellectual penetration or personal response. The bishops decided to change that.

The man they chose to lead the enterprise was John F. Kelly, a Melbourne priest. A product of the Werribee seminary, Kelly was a voracious and retentive reader. His mind was stocked with the best of the English poets and novelists, French and German theologians, Newman, Patrick White, the mystics and the historians. Yet he was also a people person— warm, funny, outgoing, encouraging, interested in *you*.

As a young priest he had been put to work in the Catholic Education Office. It was hands-on experience and he got to know teachers and pupils well and to appreciate their problems. He fought for better salaries for lay teachers, who were then few in number and often unappreciated. He started Saturday morning theology classes for religion teachers whose formal education might have been deficient. He targeted the Jansenism which was then rife in convent schools and encouraged a sane appreciation of sexuality.

As part of this campaign against Jansenism he developed pre-Cana conferences for engaged couples. For these he tapped into the Young Christian Worker movement, which he had known since its early days. It was typical of John F. Kelly that he was quick to recognise the significance of the YCW, the outstanding lay movement of the 20th century. He became one of its back-room auxiliaries.

Fulfilling the commission from the bishops to produce new catechisms took him over a decade. All across Australia teachers and education offices responded to his call for suggestions and improvements. No one-man-band, it was a communal enterprise by the Catholic teachers of Australia. As well, Kelly was in touch with overseas catechetical institutes. He showed true humility in being willing to learn from anyone; and showed some surprise when the experts at Belgium's Lumen Vitae Centre said they had learned from him.

Under the inspiration of Kelly's catechisms, religion in school became an experience rather than a subject to be studied. Through Bible and liturgy the students would be caught up in the saving power of Jesus. The emphasis on the Bible was an especially noticeable feature. Kelly urged teachers to follow Jesus even in his pedagogic methods.

Published while the Second Vatican Council was in process, these catechism texts were a first fruit of conciliar achievement. In fact, they show that Vatican II ratified initiatives and insights that were already there when the council's bishops assembled in 1962. In many ways John F. Kelly had anticipated the teaching of Vatican II. The Sydney faculty of theology recognised his worth by granting him an honorary doctorate—the only one in its history.

Then, his catechetical work done, he became a parish priest. The bishops called him back in 1973 to establish the National Pastoral Institute, an educational institute for the experienced. Here, said one of the bishops, 'he was able to encourage and enthuse and help others to appreciate and develop their gifts'.

But it was parish work which brought all of his magnificent qualities to a second flowering. He had a sacramental approach to everyday eating and drinking—as one of his obituarists said, 'he was a person who knew how to celebrate life'.

Even in death there was a final life-affirming, anti-Jansenist lesson: he left money in his will for his friends and parishioners to hold a party, at which he suggested they enjoy some malt whisky.

Images of faith

HANS & HILDE KNORR

APART FROM THE ABORIGINAL SECTIONS, there aren't many religious works in Australian art galleries. This is because the artists who came to Australia years ago and the art works available for purchase here were chiefly from the post-religious era of European art.

World War II changed that. It sent to Australia many talented artists imbued with the traditional religious cultures of central Europe. The war also eroded fashionable beliefs in materialism, freeing artists to explore religious themes.

In 1967 a small book appeared called *Religious Art in Australia* . It spotlit the emergence of religious painters and sculptors in Australia since the war. *Religious Art in Australia* provoked much debate in intellectual circles and the book soon sold out. Its appearance was a milestone in the story of Australian art. It was also a milestone in the lives of its authors, Hilde and Hans Knorr, for it was a public recognition of their separate but complementary talents.

First, Hans Knorr. Born in Bavaria, he came to Australia as a prisoner of war and stayed here when the war ended. He made a living by carving lampstands, but religious sculpture was his first love. Individual pieces, such as Madonnas, attracted attention. In 1956 he completed his first large commissions, a life-size crucifix corpus and a Madonna for St Bernard's Church, East Coburg, in Victoria. Since then, his work has gone to all parts of Australia and New Zealand.

His wife, Hilde, was born in rural Gippsland and trained as a violinist. Her marriage to a struggling artist introduced her to a life even more precarious than that of a music student. There were compensations, however, because people warmed to her husband and she met many interesting friends, such as the composer Dr Percy Jones, Catholic intellectuals at Melbourne University and the commune dwellers at Whitlands, a sort of lay monastery in the mountains northeast of Melbourne.

Life was never easy. Priests who commissioned work seemed to think that because the Knorrs were Catholics they should work for next to nothing. Erratic book-keeping didn't help, either. Once, for example, a priory paid them £45 for three figures—the friars thought the Knorrs had said £45 for the *three*, while the Knorrs thought they had said £45 for *each figure*.

The family got by on hand-me-down clothes patched and stitched together over the years. One day at Mass, Hans knelt down to pray and his patched trousers finally gave up, ripping noisily above the kneeline. Poverty had its good moments, too, as when they came back from an outing to find a parcel from Myer's. Inside was a beautiful Harris tweed overcoat with an anonymous note: 'Please accept this as a tribute to your outstanding craftsmanship'.

The Knorr children grew up aware of an oddity in their lives: their father was an artist and therefore different from their schoolfellows' dads who did regular jobs; worse, he was a German, just like the baddies in the movies and TV shows (not that the Knorrs had television). That oddity in itself was a useful preparation for life.

They lived in the Dandenongs, on a wooded hillside where Hans had space to work. Hilde ran the art gallery they opened there and baked scones for the afternoon teas the gallery served. All the time her artistic talent, which had found an early outlet in music, was drumming to be heard again. So she began to write.

Her early writings appeared in the *Messenger of the Sacred heart* and then the *Age* and the *Australian*. In all, she has published five books of fiction, as well as poetry, history and art criticism. Her autobiography, *Journey with a Stranger*, is one of her best works. Subtitled 'The Love Story of an Artist and a Writer', it is a sensitive account of how she and Hans found each other and together experienced the first wave of religious art in modern Australia.

Singing in stone

TOM BASS

THE LOGO FOR THE ST VINCENT DE PAUL SOCIETY is one of the most recognisable Catholic signs in Australia. It shows three hands and a cup. One hand offers the cup, another receives it and the third, which carries a deep wound, is blessing the exchange. The wounded hand is Christ's and the logo expresses his commission to the SVP Society: 'As often as you give a cup of water in My name, you give it to Me?'.

The design was done by sculptor Tom Bass nearly 40 years ago when he was a member of the SVP conference at Minto parish in the country south of Sydney. It is now used all over the world. Driving in Turkey, Bass saw it on a collection bin. He says today that he regards it as one of the really important things he has done.

Bass carved his way into the church. One day early in the 1950s an architect came to the art school where he was teaching and enquired whether anyone was interested in attempting a crucifix for the Jesuits' Canisius College at Pymble. The sculptor said he would try. The resulting art work shows a Christ who is triumphing over death, almost ready to ascend to his Father. In a personal quirk, Bass gave his Christ the head of an idealistic ex-Communist with whom he was then arguing.

His next crucifix was for the front wall of St Augustine's Church, Yass (NSW). This is a war memorial church, so he put a heavy weight of suffering into his Christ, who looks like a survivor of the Burma railway or some POW camp. It is a startling piece of public sculpture in a country town, which continues to draw visitors.

Inside the church there is a statue of St Paul. It shows Paul working at his trade as a sail-maker, stitching a sail which drapes over his knees. The fall of the cloth resembles the walls and roof of a church, as the sculptor suggests that Paul is stitching together the church with the strong twine of his theology. His Romanesque robes suggest Paul's episcopal leadership; while his sandalled feet recall his pastoral journeyings. This is a virile yet visionary St Paul.

We know what was in the sculptor's mind as he worked on this statue because week by week he exchanged letters with the pastor of Yass, Dr Guilford Young, who was about to become Archbishop of Hobart. Published in the *Messenger of the Sacred Heart,* the letters are a rare document in the history of sacred art in Australia. At breakfast each morning the Bass family would listen to a reading from St Paul on ABC radio and then, with all that biblical teaching in his mind, Tom would go to work on his sculpture.

In his memoirs Tom Bass recalls the impact Guilford Young made on him. He was, he writes, like a Renaissance prince; yet they met as equals. The bishop knew his theology demanded expression in formal, visible art; and the self-educated, vaguely Protestant artist sought ideas to enliven his art forms. All his life he had wanted to carve totems—sculptures that would give back to people the ideas that mattered to them. His was public art, not for private galleries.

Drawn into the church, Bass used his art to meditate on the great truths of Christianity. Thus a commission for the baptismal font in the church at Camperdown, an inner suburb of Sydney, led him to explore themes of death and resurrection with Christ. Next door, at Sancta Sophia College, the Sacré Coeur nuns had him sculpt a votive figure of the Sacred Heart. For Hobart cathedral he did an expressive statue of Our Lady as archetype of the church. Not solely a religious artist, he won major commissions for wall sculptures on public buildings, such as the National Library of Australia in Canberra, and sculptures in Melbourne streets and gardens.

As the 1960s drew to their close, Tom Bass felt less comfortable as a Catholic. The strident anti-Communism of the time sickened him; as did the way pro-government bishops penalised priests who opposed the Vietnam War. In a statement to the press he announced the withdrawal from church membership of himself and his family. Nevertheless, he has gone on producing public art for Catholic patrons. And his logo for the St Vincent de Paul Society remains as a recognisable legacy of his years as a Catholic.

The one thing needful

EILEEN FRAWLEY

MOST PEOPLE DO NOT FEAR DEATH; it's *dying* they worry about. How you face up to the process of dying says a lot about the sort of person you are. For some people, the period before death is the high point of their life, revealing them as giants of the human spirit, perhaps even as saints.

Such a person was Eileen Frawley. She died in 1981, aged 46. Fifteen years earlier she had come to Mount Olivet Hospital, at Newness in Brisbane, in an advanced stage of multiple sclerosis. For the rest of her life the hospital was her home.

Within a short time she could do little on her own: she could speak, turn her head, hold something very light for a few moments and operate a tongue switch to call the nurses.

Although she couldn't get to it, she knew where everything was in her bedside locker. Teased about all the things in the locker, she would reply, 'Well, just you try and move all your things from a houseful to a lockerful'.

In the top drawer there was money for newspapers, gambling tickets, tissues, her address book and a dictionary for crossword puzzles. Another drawer held her filing system of birthdays and anniversaries. She had cards to send for every occasion: birthdays, babies, anniversaries, feast days, deaths.

She bought the morning and evening papers, scouring them for news of her hometown, Ipswich, and the people she knew. An avid radio listener, she was first with the news, whether it was a fire or a bargain sale.

Although she was dying slowly, Eileen Frawley was more interested in other people than herself.The staff at Brisbane's Mater Hospital, where she had been earlier, always remembered the effect she had had on a girl in the bed next to her.

Bitter about events in her own life, the girl could not understand Eileen's cheerfulness and acceptance of her illness. Gradually, however, Eileen Frawley's conversation about the love of God softened the girl's bitterness. The same sort of thing happened at Mount Olivet: people who had terminal cancer, for example, would be wheeled over to do the crossword with her and they would draw strength from her. She became a spiritual resource for the whole hospital.

What was her secret? Part of it was that she had very little self regard. She was more interested in other people than herself—hence the newspapers, the radio and the cards.

A greater part of the secret of her serenity was religious: she accepted her illness as God's will for her and turned it to good account. Like St Paul, she could say, 'I rejoice in my sufferings for your sake, and in my flesh I make up what is lacking in Christ's sufferings for the sake of his body, the Church'.

Not that she thought her multiple sclerosis could add anything to the redemptive work of Christ. But, as St Paul taught, it could reveal again and make present the innocent suffering by which Christ saved humanity.

Sr Edna Skewes RSC understood this when she wrote of Eileen Frawley, 'This was to be her vocation, to give herself entirely to God with whatever suffering this might entail. She went even further, and made a redemptive offering of her life as a prayer for the world's people, and for the saving of souls, in union with the suffering and death of Christ on the cross'.

So Eileen had Mass said in thanksgiving for all these blessings in her life. And when, towards the end, she began to deteriorate, she tried to tell her nurses by signs that she was not worried or afraid.

Her death, when it came, was of a piece with her years of redemptive suffering. A cousin, a Mercy sister, sat by the bedside saying the rosary. Then she took the dying woman's hand and whispered into her ear that her work was done.

The Mercy sister said the words of Christ on the cross: 'I have done all that you asked me to do. It is finished'. At these words of the Lord, Eileen Frawley became still, her tense neck muscles relaxed, her breathing quietened; there was calm, peace, even radiance, until the end. Her offering had been accepted, her life was complete.

And so she died.

Spreading the word

KATIE MOTUM

CATECHISTS WHO TEACH RELIGION IN STATE SCHOOLS have opened a new chapter in the story of Australian Catholics. Numbered in thousands, they have taken responsibility for one of the central missions of the church, handing on the faith. In teaching, they have strengthened and deepened their own appreciation of the faith. The boom in adult education and the growth of Catholic publishing in Australia are direct results of this—the thousands of catechists have created a demand for intellectual nourishment. This is the story of one such catechist.

Kathleen Noela Motum came from a working class family. When she was young her parents split up so she had to take a hand in rearing her younger brother. When she was barely 16, a commonwealth scholarship got her to Sydney University, where she would in time graduate BA, Dip Ed.

This was in the mid-1950s, the hey-day of the Newman Society. She became an enthusiastic member, known to all as

Katie. A Newman songbook she edited survives from those days, a sunny testament to the untroubled student Catholicism of Newman members.

Inspired by chaplain Fr Roger Pryke and lay leaders such as John Dormer, the Newmans anticipated much of the teaching of Vatican II. Energised by the liturgy, their spirituality was based on the gospels, which they encountered in regular group discussions. They accepted their baptismal responsibility for witnessing to Christ in the university. Theirs was not a political Catholicism, aimed at taking over or colonising the university. Rather, they sought to serve the university as an intellectual centre.

In those years, Australian university students were becoming more and more aware of Asia. The Colombo Plan had brought many Asian students to our universities, so, unlike most other Australians of that time, students knew and were friends with Asians. They thus became prime activists against discriminatory policies, such as the White Australia policy. Herb Feith, a political science student at Melbourne University, was active in promoting student awareness of Asia. Graduating in 1951, he found his way to Indonesia, where he got work in the ministry of information. Unlike other westerners, Feith worked at local rates of pay and lived with Indonesians. From his experience grew a volunteer scheme that attracted many Australian Christians willing to serve in Indonesia.

Katie Motum got to hear about it and she and her friend Joan Minogue volunteered to teach on local pay. They landed in Jakarta with 11 heavy items of luggage and took the first train by a circuitous route to their posting in the interior. They had read about railway thieves, so one of them always stayed awake to guard their luggage. Katie clutched an umbrella as a weapon and when they were off-loaded at Jogjakarta she spread herself across the luggage, rapping the knuckles of porters who tried to commandeer their belongings. Later they would laugh at themselves; but at the time they felt very much on their own.

Soon the two young women had settled into their new society. As with most Australians, their severest privation was the lack of solitude. The work was satisfying, teaching English at the teachers college. After three years Joan would marry there, becoming Mrs Hardjono. Katie also married, but back in Australia, to Alan Powell, a PhD student she had met in the Newman Society.

By the end of the 1960s they were living in Melbourne with their four children and Katie had joined the parish Confraternity of Christian Doctrine (CCD) as a catechist. A stay in the US enabled her to sharpen her catechetical skills. When they came home to Melbourne the parish priest of Ringwood offered her a post as coordinator of the CCD in the parish. In time the Ringwood CCD program became known as the best in the archdiocese.

Hungry for deeper knowledge, Katie enrolled at the Yarra Theological Union where, studying part-time, she earned a Bachelor of Theology degree. Her grades were all credits and distinctions. Then the Catholic Education Office created a new post for the CCD at headquarters and appointed her to it. This made her very happy because it showed that the CCD had come of age in the archdiocese.

By this time, however, she knew there was something seriously wrong with her health, which chemotherapy could not avert. She died on the morning of 11 April 1984. Katie Motum Powell was typical of the new breed of selfreliant women who are changing the story of Catholic Australia.

The way to freedom

SHEILA CASSIDY

Sydney people still remember Sheila Cassidy from the time, in the mid-1950s, when she studied medicine there. After two years she transferred to Oxford and her Sydney friends lost track of her.

Then, at the end of 1975, they were amazed to read about her in the papers. After an honours degree at Oxford and further qualification as a surgeon, she had gone to Chile to work as a doctor in a local clinic. Her practice exposed her to the hard lives of the poor and showed her the injustice of a society heavily weighted in favour of the rich. She came to appreciate and love the priests and nuns who were sharing the lives of the poor.

She felt too their apprehension when a military coup over-threw the Allende socialist government in 1973. Immediately army trucks began to forage through the mean streets of the poorer suburbs. Bodies of labour leaders and leftists began to float down the river. She continued her work.

Called by a priest to dig a bullet out of a wounded revolutionary's leg, Sheila Cassidy crossed the line of legalitv. There was really nothing else a decent doctor could do. Nevertheless, she had crossed the line.

A week later the secret police arrested her. They stripped her and tied her to a metal bed and ran electricity over her while questioning her. She told them lies. When they found this out, they put her back on the bed, clipped an extra electrode to her vagina and turned up the voltage. Eventually, she told them what they wanted to know.

The next two months were spent in prison. Here she was, a respected British doctor, daughter of an Australian Rhodes Scholar and an artistic English gentlewoman, suddenly dispossessed, powerless, unfree. Later she would say that what she remembered most was fear—fear of pain, of helplessness, of brutality, of death.

Alone, in solitary confinement, she turned to God. Her first instinct was to bargain with him, begging him to secure her release. Then came the thought: Don't hold out your empty hands to God in supplication, but in offering. Powerless and a captive, she had still one freedom: she could abandon herself into the hands of God. 'Here I am, Lord, take me. I trust you. Do with me what you will.'

She learnt another lesson in prison: not all the good people are in the church. The centuries of Latin American collaboration between churchmen and the ruling classes had given religion a sour taste in many mouths. Her fellow prisoners rejected religion but were passionate about justice and abundant in their generosity. Like the early Christians, they shared what they had with each other. Once, for example, Sheila's hair kept falling over her face. She asked if anyone had a hairclip and was immediately given one. Weeks later, she found out that it was the only hairclip her donor had.

At last, diplomatic intervention got her out of prison and on to a plane to England. Her story made world headlines. What next? Off and on, she had thought of entering a convent. For 18 months she tried an enclosed order; but it didn't work out. God had other plans for Dr Sheila Cassidy.

He drew her to Plymouth, to become medical director of St Luke's Hospice. Caring for the dying in a hospice drains the carers, for they must respond to the whole complex of human needs of those they serve. Sheila's Chilean discovery of abandonment to God's will as a way forward to freedom has stood by her in the hospice.

The dying are as powerless as prisoners. They can come to accept what is happening to them, not as a giving up of the struggle, but as a letting go in order to grow. In this perspective, they are like the little group who stood round the cross with Jesus as he abandoned himself to his Father's will.

Death isn't meant to be easy and life isn't easy for the hospice carers. They learn from their mistakes. There are, of course, special moments that act like a grace of encouragement. Sheila treasures the memory of a difficult woman who announced that she had been planning her own funeral. 'It's got to be a party', said the doctor impulsively. 'Death's the beginning, not the end.' The impulse proved right. The woman gripped her hand and replied, 'You give me such strength when you talk like that'. The following week she died peacefully.

A poet's confidence in God

JAMES McAULEY

ONCE SEEN, JAMES McAULEY WAS NEVER FORGOTTEN. His seamed and riven face printed itself on your memory. It was the face of a battler; although the battles McAuley fought were not backlane affairs of fist and bottle, they were battles of ideas. He was a militant of Catholic conservatism.

He came into the church through the library. From his teens a voracious reader, he once said that his real education at Sydney University had come, not from any of the professors, but from its great Fisher Library. The city's municipal library was also acknowledged as a potent educational force: 'that true *alma mater* of mine,' he called it. There, for example, he borrowed one after the other volumes of Sir James Frazer's *Golden Bough*, a comparative religion classic which destroyed his boyhood Anglican Christianity.

He still went to church, however, because he was in the choir and an enthusiastic organist. During his university years

209

he supported himself with regular jobs as a church organist. At university too, he blossomed as a jazz pianist, in demand for student revues and parties. Knowing that he could become a good classical pianist, but not a great one, he decided to look elsewhere for his life's work.

By this time, he knew he wanted to be a poet. At high school he had published poetry in the school magazine but it was university which consolidated his talent. He was *the* university poet of his time, the one everyone read and discussed. University gave him the necessary time and space to think about poetry. To earn a living, he would become a teacher; but his vocation was to be a poet.

World War II saw him drafted into an unconventional think-tank which operated somewhere between the prime minister's department and the military higher command. One leisurely afternoon he and another poet in uniform concocted a series of hoax poems, which they attributed to a Sydney garage hand, 'Ern Malley'. The hoax duped a leading literary editor and scandalised modernist literary circles. Some of them never forgave McAuley.

By now, the think-tank had directed his attention to Australia's post-war responsibilities in Papua New Guinea. Here, waiting to be experienced, were the primitive societies he had previously only read about in anthropological texts such as *The Golden Bough*. He came to see that in many ways these societies were more integrated, more colourful and more truly human than the secularised and atomised society he knew at home.

As he reflected on this new experience McAuley began to think that what bound PNG societies together and gave them meaning was their religion. Religion acknowledged a presence beyond the here and now and deferred to it. Without religion, Western society was in danger of falling apart. Thus by a combination of experience, reflection and reading he found his way to the Catholic Church in 1951.

Back in Sydney in one of the new parishes set up after the war, he played the harmonium at Sunday Mass and so met another parishioner with a young family, Richard Connolly. They formed a close friendship and began to write hymns together. In time these hymns would revolutionise Catholic worship, because they brought an Australian voice to the liturgy.

McAuley supported the change to English in the Mass but in later years came to regret the extent of innovation. It is easy to pull down but harder to build with integrity of form and style, he said. Musically there had been an immense loss. The liturgical waste seemed matched by much else that was going wrong in the church. In self defence, he stopped reading modern theologians, did not look at the church papers and spoke to priests only if they were personal friends.

Yet these years were filled with creative work. His magazine, *Quadrant*, had a distinctive voice which no one ignored. His political alliance with B.A. Santamaria had its ups and downs but it was a real presence in Australian life, not a sideshow. In 1961 he moved to the University of Tasmania and thus found time for important works of literary criticism.

Before he died of cancer in 1976, he wrote an essay for *Quadrant* which, while candid about the human cost of belonging to the church, nonetheless witnessed to the survival of his religious convictions. His final poems were serene and faith-filled. Between optimism and pessimism—he liked to say, quoting the saintly Archbishop de Boismenu of Papua New Guinea, who had attracted him into the church—there is confidence in God.

Continuing the tradition

Sr IRENE McCORMACK

She had returned home from the day's work, changed her clothes, watered the garden, brought in the day's washing and was thinking of what to get for the evening meal, when someone started banging on her front door and shouting for her. Snatching up a wind jacket, she hurried to the door.

Come with us, the people there ordered. Now. Immediately. Since they had guns in their hands, she obeyed. They marched her to the village square, calling on the villagers to assemble there. She looked ahead of her and prayed to withstand whatever the future might bring.

In the square she found four of the men who gave leadership and direction to her village. Their 'trial' had already begun. What were their crimes? One was the acting mayor, another had been deputy mayor, another had organised the purchase of a satellite dish to bring TV to the village.

To their captors they were dangerous because they made present life possible. That was their crime. For the captors belonged to an ultra leftist movement, known as the Shining Path, which aimed to destroy everything so that they could rebuild the world according to their own plans. It was perverse, even psychotic, and quite random in its violence.

And this woman? What was her crime? Irene McCormack was a Josephite sister who had come from Australia to the mountain village of Huasahuasi in the Andes mountains of Peru. She organised cooking and sewing classes for women and play groups for children, ran a little library and taught parents how to catechise their children, and for the hungry she supervised a communal kitchen where the main dish was potato soup. Such were her crimes.

So the Shining Path guerrillas marched her to the square and abused her for an hour. There were from 60 to 80 of them, all armed, some as young as ten or twelve. The young ones seemed to be on drugs. They said she was a Yankee imperialist and when Huasahuasi people shouted back that no, she wasn't, she was an Australian, they said it didn't matter. She had given food to the poor—that was her crime.

Throughout this harangue Irene sat on a seat at the fountain, facing her accusers. The other captives lay on the ground. Then she too was ordered to lie on the ground. A Shining Path guerrilla, believed to be a young girl, came up to her and shot her in the back of the head. Other shots followed. And the men were shot too. The date was 21 May 1991.

The death of Irene McCormack was soon known in Australia. The response to the news was overwhelming—newspaper reports and editorials, words in parliament, requiem Masses, memorials and reminiscences from those who had known her. What emerged was a picture of an Australian religious sister who somehow seemed familiar even to those who had never met her.

Irene McCormack had grown up in the Western Australian bush, gone to Catholic schools and there found a vocation to the Josephites. After school, she waited for a year before entering the convent, a year filled with the usual pursuits of a teenager: picnics, parties and sport.

After novitiate and teacher training in the east, she returned to the west, serving for the most part in rural schools. In time she became the principal of Kearnen College at Manjimup. To counter the stress of her work, she took up golf, a game she enjoyed. An avid Australian Rules fan since her youth, she was a loyal barracker for the local team.

But economic and demographic pressures were closing country schools one by one. Now in her late forties, Irene considered how she should use the rest of her life. The withdrawal from bush schools saddened her because that is where Mary MacKillop had started. Still, different times, different initiatives. When word got round of a plan to send some Josephites to work in the hill country of Peru, she put up her hand.

Once the Australian bush had been the frontier for Josephites; now it was the third world. So, even if her death was unique, Irene McCormack's life was true to the MacKillop tradition. Any one of her sisters could have been where she was on the evening of 21 May 1991. That is the glory of the Josephites.

A life for teachers

ANN CLARK

Ann Clark died in January 1997, aged 61, and her death drew obituaries in the national press. Head of Catholic education in Parramatta diocese for ten years, she had been the first woman to lead a church school system in NSW. She was a symbol of the new lay leadership emerging in Australian Catholicism.

Ann was a prayerful woman, able to speak easily of religious matters. Like many of her Vatican II generation of Australian Catholics, she made the Bible the wellspring of her spirituality. Environmentally conscious, she often drew the images of her prayers from nature. Praying with a group, she used photographic slides and recorded music. Long association with the Sisters of Charity, as a pupil at St Vincent's College, Potts Point (NSW) and then as a teacher in their schools, gave her facility in religious affairs.

At the end of her life, already stricken with ovarian cancer, she acknowledged some of her debt to the Sisters of Charity by travelling to Victoria and speaking to teachers at their St Columba's College, Essendon. It was a typical Ann Clark address, alive with faith and hope and belief in the power of teachers to make a difference in society.

She told her audience that by its very nature teaching is about hope and future promise, its focus on growth and development. Catholics, she said, are resurrection people, so their schools should equip young women to transform society. Graduates of St Columba's College should be women of

> *competence*: able to contribute to society;
> *conscience*: formed by gospel values and Catholic faith;
> *commitment*: loving Christian faith and practising it in the Catholic tradition;
> *compassion*: speaking for the voiceless and valuing cultural and religious diversity.

She was in demand as a speaker at conferences and in-service seminars across Australia and overseas. Audiences wanted to hear Ann Clark because she gave them a vision they could believe in. A frequent theme was the difference good teachers could make in achieving a just society. One of her last addresses, to the Australian College of Education, was titled 'Our Teachers—the Greatest Gift'. That said it all.

On the other hand, she did not think that teachers could do it all themselves. Instead of a 'fortress school', where teachers did everything and kept others out, she said she wanted an 'involved school'. She meant a school where teachers, priests, parents and students all had a say in what went on. She set up a Parent Representative Council to involve parents in decision making.

In dealing with priests of the Parramatta diocese she was direct, tactful and astute. When problems came up, she would go to clergy meetings and discuss them frankly. Even those who opposed her agenda admired her integrity and professionalism. They knew she wanted what was best for the school-children. Whatever the opposition, she very much wanted the priests of the diocese involved in decision making about the schools.

In this, too, she was a Vatican II woman. Co-responsibility had been a watchword of the conciliar generation, who spoke often of collegiality in the church. They wanted a church which involved everyone and for which everyone was responsible, not just the priests. This is the sort of language Parramatta Catholics are used to hearing because, following the leadership given by Bishop Bede Heather, theirs is a diocese which consciously tries to make the Vatican II vision come to life.

The word 'vision' often appeared in Ann Clark's talks. In New York she photographed an optician's advertisement that read, 'Vision is the art of seeing the invisible'. That became an overhead projection picture in an address to Brisbane school principals. Leaders are people with vision, she told them.

Many honours came to Ann Clark, some of them heavy with responsibilities. Among them was her appointment by successive NSW governments to the board of the University of Western Sydney. She accepted this extra task because she believed that only the best was good enough for the educational community in the western suburbs. Ill health made her unable to complete a PhD exploring how people like teachers could become 'transformational' leaders. So she was delighted when her university made her an honorary doctor.

At her funeral Ann's husband placed the doctoral bonnet on the coffin. It was an exquisite moment, friends knew, which brought together both private and public lives of a woman who thought teachers were the most important people in society and so gave her life to them.

Great Australian Catholics
An alphabetical list